Fairies at work and at play

Fairies at work and at play

observed by
Geoffrey Hodson

Quest Books
Theosophical Publishing House
Wheaton, Illinois * Chennai, India

Copyright © The Theosophical Publishing House

First Quest Edition 1982
Fifth Printing 2021

All rights reserved. No part of this book may be reproduced
in any manner except for quotations embodied in critical
articles or reviews. For additional information write to

Quest Books
Theosophical Publishing House
P.O. Box 270
Wheaton, IL 60187-0270

www.questbooks.com

Library of Congress Cataloging-in-Publication Data
Hodson, Geoffrey.
Fairies at work and play.
1. Fairies   I. Title.
BF1552.H62   1982   001.9   81-53009
ISBN 978-0-8356-0553-3

Printed in the United States of America

CONTENTS

ACKNOWLEDGMENT

I WISH to express my gratitude for and appreciation of the great help I have received from some of my fellow members of the T.S. in writing this book.

PREFACE

"I CAN corroborate in detail many of the descriptions of nature-spirits given by Mr. Hodson, and find myself entirely in harmony with the general atmosphere conveyed. Frequently little touches occur which show unmistakably to a brother clairvoyant that the writer has seen what he is describing. Perpetually points emerge which recall my own investigations many years ago. Mr. Hodson seems to have devoted himself chiefly to the beautiful tiny creatures who engage themselves almost entirely in work for the vegetable kingdom, and he gives an admirable account of their proceedings. He sees less frequently the larger beings, often approaching human size, to whom I have devoted my attention when examining fairy life.

"Mr. Hodson has caught most admirably the pre-eminently joyous tone of the life of the nature-spirits. They live so thoroughly in union with the divine intention; desire in them never seems to conflict with it as it so often does with us. I agree thoroughly with Mr. Hodson as to the general differences observable between the average land-fairy and the average sea-fairy. I happen to have before me all day long in my southern home a glorious view of land and sea closely intermingled, and I constantly pause for a moment to watch just such activities as are described in these articles.

"Mr. Hodson is much to be congratulated in that he possesses by nature the faculties for which most of us have had to labour so long and so hard. May the day soon come when such faculties shall be more common, and when humanity makes that much of advancement we shall understand God's plan far better, and therefore we shall see how to mould our lives more intelligently with His Will.

" Such articles as these do much good in widening men's conceptions and showing them a little more of the wondrous and glorious ocean of manifested life on all planes in the midst of which we live our little day—a day that is marvellously brightened by the knowledge which clairvoyance can give." (Extract from a letter written by Bishop Leadbeater, after reading certain chapters of this book published serially in *The Herald of the Star*.)

FAIRIES AT WORK AND AT PLAY

INTRODUCTION

It is essential to offer to the general reader some explanation of the phenomena described by Mr. Hodson in this work. Without an indication as to their place in the scheme of things the observations recorded will read like fantasy. They may still remain that to many sceptical minds, but the least that those of us can do who know these records to be genuine is to offer a rational explanation of the material presented which will be at least intelligible to a logical mind, if not entirely convincing.

Science recognises in the varying rates of vibration of the ether the cause of all " material," both in the visible and invisible world of physical experience. Solids, liquids, and gases are the three familiar states of physical matter. Ether is postulated as the fourth, and through this as medium heat and light play—each with a known series of wavelengths. Electricity also has as its field this fourth region of physical matter, a region which, it is suspected, has also its sub-divisions.

The ancient tradition buried at the heart of all great religions, and known to-day as the mystery tradition, or occultism, extends the idea of matter at varying rates of vibration still further, and recognises matter

11

at a rate too fine to be measured or tested by any physical means. This manifestation, no longer physical, is still substantial; that is, it can take a form, and acts according to discoverable laws. It is so subtle that the currents of feeling and emotion affect it; hence it is called emotional, or, technically, "astral" matter. It has a large variety of phenomena associated with it, which have been to some extent measured and described in this same mystery teaching. Beyond the astral world there stretches yet another range of experience, the mental, and beyond that others of a still finer nature, responding to still more spiritual aspects of consciousness. All these rates of vibration interpenetrate each other, in the same way that solids, liquids and gases are all present in a sponge filled with water— the sponge being solid, the water liquid, and the gases themselves composing the water. So our physical world has, around and within it, astral and mental activities running close knit to its own, and intimately associated with its phenomena. The phenomena of "life"—such as cell growth, variations of structure, sports, etc., the causes of which are so little known— are due to influences from the subtler worlds, as we shall presently see. No wonder, then, that they confound the student who is blind to all save physical rates of activity.

It is possible to investigate these subtler rates, though, in order to do this, organs of perception must first be developed. The organs of perception of these finer levels of experience must each be tuned to respond to the order of material which they are meant to investigate. In practice, such mechanisms are only found in a specially disciplined body. Human nature is exactly fitted for such study, for the human being is not limited to the physical body which we see, but has at each level a " body " or vehicle of expression, made of the material of that plane. So occultism teaches that each human soul uses a physical body, including the finer levels of the physical ether, as well as solids, liquids and gases, and also an astral or emotional body and a mental vehicle.

As the physical structure becomes more refined and delicately organised through the long processes of evolution, these subtler bodies also become more highly developed, and begin to specialise organs of perception at their own levels. This is the basis of clairvoyance* as it is now familiarly called—an experience which ranges from a transitory " vision " in a moment of strain, through the experience of the partially developed organ, which can see occasionally but cannot direct its sight to any extent, to the point of full self-conscious control of the inner vision. In the latter case it can be used at its own level as we use vision at the physical level. Even then the phenomena of these worlds are very elusive, as Mr. Hodson's records prove from time to time. Their motion or vibration is so comparatively rapid, their laws of activity so subtle, compared with the physical world, that words fail to describe what is seen, and the vision often fails to record all that one might wish to know of any given fact.

The public is fortunate in having before it, in this book, a record of observations made by a clairvoyant who, while undoubtedly gifted with sight at the physical etheric, astral and, to some extent at any rate, at higher levels, is as frank in regard to his limitations as he is honest in the application of his gifts. Mr. Hodson will

---

* Clairvoyance should not be confused with mediumship or trance conditions. *We speak here of clairvoyance only.*

often admit his inability to push his observations further, as well as his lack of *entire* comprehension of what he sees. He noted down, in most instances on the spot, the forms and activities which he observed, and his statements have independent corroboration from many sources.*

And what is it that he has observed? A vast variety of etheric and astral forms, large and small, working together in organised co-operation on what we must call the *life* side of Nature, stimulating growth, bringing colour to the flowers, brooding over beautiful spots, playing in waves and waterfalls, dancing in the wind and the sunlight—in fact, another order of evolution running parallel to and blended with our own.

Common tradition has always recognised its existence, and, in every byway of the world where hearts are clean and minds are simple, stories of the " little people " abound.†   Here we have before us a record of researches running over some years, which confirms that common tradition in many details.

The mystery teaching again fills in the gaps and makes of broken fragments an intelligible theory. The *deva* ‡ evolution is said to run in partnership with our humanity. In the development of the earlier forms, mineral, vegetable, animal, the Nature-spirits, *devas*, fairies or elementals (to give them a few of their many names) lead the way. Their work is the evolution of beautiful and responsive forms. When humanity reaches maturity and develops its inner faculties, the direction of

* For further discussion of the validity of such phenomena, see *Fairies*, by E. L. Gardner.

† See *Fairy Faith in Celtic Countries*, by Wentz.

‡ *Deva*, a Sanskrit term meaning " shining ones "; it includes all orders of nature-spirits, angels and the lesser gods.

Nature's activities begins to fall into its hands. We can see this beginning to-day in the agricultural world.

During the latter half of the evolutionary cycle, humanity, having come to an understanding of the natural principles of growth, conquers Nature by obeying her fundamental laws, and thereby wins the willing obedience of the lower orders of nature-spirits and the joyous co-operation of the higher ranks of invisible workers.

Though the sceptical mind of the age may question the validity of such evidence, the open mind will pursue this fascinating quest, full of such promise for the world's welfare. The occultist sees no " dead matter " anywhere —every stone thrills with life, every jewel has its attendant consciousness, however minute. The grass and trees are pulsing to the touch of tiny workers, whose magnetic bodies act as the matrix in which miracles of growth and colour become possible.

As the following observations and remarks by Mr. Hodson bear directly on this point, they are inserted here rather than in the body of the book: —

"In the examination of bulbs growing in bowls, it is observed that large numbers of small sub-microscopic etheric creatures are moving about in and around the growing plants. They are visible etherically as points of light, playing around the stems and passing in and out of the growing plant. They have the power to rise into the air to a height equal to that of the plant, but I have not seen any rise further than that. They absorb something from the atmosphere, re-enter the tissue of the plant and discharge it. This process is going on continually, the creatures are entirely self-absorbed, sufficiently self-conscious to experience a dim sense of well-being and to feel affection for the plant, which they regard as their body. They have no consciousness apart from this.

When the process of absorbing is taking place they become enlarged and appear like pale violet or lilac-coloured spheres, some two inches in diameter, with radii of force flowing from a central point within the sphere. The ends of these lines extend slightly beyond the circumference. Having expanded to the largest size which they are able to reach, they return close to the plant, enter it, and begin to discharge the material, or vital force, which they have absorbed. The natural etheric vital flow from the half-grown plants reaches quite two feet above them, and in it other tiny creatures play and dance, tossed up and down by the flowing force in which they rejoice. To etheric sight they are less than a quarter of an inch in size, though both varieties must be sub-microscopic from the point of view of solid measurement.

In addition to this a process of absorption by the plants themselves is plainly visible, etheric matter flowing towards them from all sides. In some cases feebly waving tentacles are extended from the etheric double of the plant, and through them etheric matter is being absorbed. These tentacles are hollow etheric tubes, slightly curved and slightly wider at the mouth, and are pale grey in colour. The longest I can see extends four to six inches from the plant and is from a quarter to half an inch in diameter.

The little nature-spirits do not confine their energies, apparently, to one plant, or even to one

bowl—for I see them flitting about from one bowl
to another. The bulbs themselves give the impression of great power and concentrated energy. They
are quite like power-houses charged with great force.
The colour is pinkish-violet, with an intenser light
in the centre, and from this centre the flowing force
previously described radiates vertically upwards,
carrying with it at a much slower pace the moisture
and other nutriment.

As a result of this and other attempts to understand the processes of growth I have come to the
following conclusions: —

In the heart of every seed is a living centre, which
contains the stored-up results of previous seasons
as a vibratory possibility. Apparently the awakening,
or stirring of the life in due season produces *sound*.
This sound is heard throughout the elemental regions
where the builders answer the call to labour. Every
type of growth, whether of stem, shoot, leaf or
flower appears to have its own note, or call, to which
the appropriate nature-spirit ' builder ' must respond.
This sound also has a form-producing activity, and
is, probably, the means by which the archetypal form
is translated to the etheric level where it becomes the
etheric mould.

Some of the results of this vibration appear to
be: —

  (1) To separate and insulate a portion of the
      atmosphere round the seed.
  (2) To call the builders, who, entering the·
      specialised sphere, are enabled to materialise
      on the sub-plane in which they have to
      work.
  (3) To set the matter within the sphere vibrat-

ing, at the required rate, and to specialise it, in readiness for the work of the builders.

(4) Probably also to materialise the archetypal form into an etheric mould.

New vibrations are introduced, as leaf, shoot, stem, and flower are to be built, so that the corresponding free matter is affected, and the corresponding builder is called and set to work on the appropriate matter.

The vibration, or sound, appears to radiate, not only from the life centre, from which it first springs in due season, but also from every embyro cell. The corresponding builder absorbs the appropriate matter, *i.e.*, that which is responding to the same vibration as himself and the cell he is building, and transforms it by association with himself into a suitable condition; he changes it from free to specialised material and discharges it, atom by atom, to the cell from which the sound is being uttered, building it into the etheric model. The vibrating cell acts as a magnet and draws the newly arrived material to its appropriate position, so that the cell is gradually enlarged until it reaches its limit of possible expansion; it then divides, and a new cell is gradually built up by a repetition of the process.

While the material is in close association with the builder, it is not only specialised to suit the requirements of the cell, but it is given the light vibration to which the builder naturally responds, *i.e.*, it is coloured.

In the early stages, when only the green shoot is appearing, the builders of a certain order are employed; tiny etheric creatures, appearing as points of light. Leaf and stem seem to be the field of their labours. Each change in structure and colour calls for another set of builders.

When the flower-stem and flower are to be built, a new set of builders arrives on the scene. Apparently these are more advanced, for, on their arrival, the whole process of growth is quickened and stimulated.

They work in precisely the same way, and, as soon as coloration is to begin, the *fairies proper* appear and implant their special rate of vibration, changing the white and green into the particular colour corresponding to the note which called them and by which they work.

These last are sufficiently advanced to be fully aware of their task and to find great pleasure in its joyous performance, and they take immense pride in the growing ' child ' under their care.

They remain in close attendance, as each new petal and bud opens, until the structure is complete and the task of the builders is finished. They are conscious and appreciative of the admiration of human beings for their work; but, on our approach they seem to plead that the flower shall not be injured. If it is cut they will follow it into the room and stay with it for some time.

When the completely flowered condition is reached the full chord is sounding forth, and, could we but hear it, our gardens would have an additional joy. We do not, however, hear that chord, though it may be that, in some cases, we contact it as a scent. We may smell the sound!

As the life force is withdrawn, the notes die

down, and a reversal takes place. Processes of
great intricacy appear to begin, as, bereft of the
controlling and guiding force, the process of decay
sets in.

It is worthy of note that, in the instinctive
labour of absorption and discharge, the builders,
who are said to be on the same line of evolution as
the bees, perform a function closely analogous to
theirs when they travel abroad for honey and then
convey and discharge it into the cells of the
honeycomb."

A word must be said about the appearance of these
" builders " in all their various shapes and guises. All
the forms of the inner worlds, constituted of matter so
sensitive that it reflects the vibrations of thought and
feeling, are naturally extremely fluidic and shifting.
None of the fairies, gnomes, nor higher devas can be
said to have a fixed " solid " body, as we understand
the term. They may occasionally materialise, often
using as the basis of this materialisation the thought-
forms that peasants and children have built of them;
occasionally, as in the case of the brownie who copied
Mr. Hodson's boots (see p. 32), they imitate forms
they have seen and admired. No one who understands
a little about the laws of thought, as well as something
in regard to the nature of this order of beings and their
lack of a clearly developed mental principle, will be
surprised that the fairies of tradition and the fairies
observed clairvoyantly appear in the same garb—
wings, wands, shining stars and all. The surprise would
be if they were different. The elemental life rejoices to
jump into a ready-made thought-form as much as an
active child delights in dressing up! It will use such a

thought-form for work or play as may suit its con-
venience.

The natural " body " used by elemental lives seems to
be a pulsing globe of light. Streams of force radiating
from this centre build up floating figures, " wings " of
radiating energy, and filmy shapes of vaguely human
likeness. In the more evolved forms the head and eyes
are always clearly distinguishable, often the whole figure
is there, with a " centre " of light blazing at the heart or
head. A sylph of this type might materialise into a
beautiful male or female form for work at the etheric
level among plants, animals, or even human beings, but
its natural body is at the astral level, iridescent, changing,
pulsating with astral forces, but not limited to a fixed or
definite shape.

The account of plant growth just quoted introduces us
to the humblest order of nature-spirits at work. The
variety of forms in the deva kingdom is endless, but is
roughly classified by tradition into four groups, according
to the element in which they work. Earth, water, air and
fire spirits are called respectively gnomes, undines, sylphs
and salamanders. The gnome does not always have to
remain a gnome, however, but can progress in the course
of the centuries towards ever higher forms: after caring
for plants and trees he may ensoul the element of fire,
and, later still, may become a great angel helper in the
work of human evolution.

The consciousness of deva beings is much freer than
our human consciousness. Their mentality and sense of
responsibility vary enormously according to their development. Tiny etheric creatures working in the grass run
about aimlessly, just " going somewhere " like gnats
in the sun. The busy travelling of these specks of
etheric being has its function—that of keeping active

the vital currents in the grass itself and so stimulating growth even in that low order of plant life—but these tiny entities have only a mass consciousness, if any, of the purpose for which they exist. So also the groups of workers, brownies, elves, and pixies, seem to work at their tasks like a hive of bees or a nest of ants, without individual responsibility, though instinctively in touch with Nature's plan. The gnome and the fairy are still without an individual mind, one, that is, which would be capable of selection and discrimination in the face of equally balanced opposites: their intelligence would be comparable to that of a pet dog or domestic animal, alert and observant, though not yet rational, and this would hold good of all orders up to the devas of high mental attainment.

These workers with Nature differ from man, then, most fundamentally on this point—that humanity (however ignorant it may be of the fact) has as its centre of consciousness the mental faculty, whereas the nature-spirit has its ultimate centre of self-consciousness in the intuition. This shows itself throughout their activities in their almost unconscious sense of co-operation with others at their own level, in their willing obedience to those members of their own kingdom who are of higher rank than themselves and in their direct sense of Nature's plan for growth in all kingdoms. This direct touch with the plan consists not in an analytical knowledge, but in an unconscious recognition of its validity and a real delight in serving its purpose.

The organisation for work is a voluntary hierarchical system. The whole scheme of activities is said by tradition to be divided into seven streams. At the head of each stream stands a great archangel, one of the "seven spirits before the throne of God," and beneath him on a Jacob's ladder of development, no rung missing, stands the rank of angelic hosts, Nature's builders. The higher devas know the plan, and disseminate it by a kind of mental osmosis to all the ranks below them. Each group has its leader, responsible to one of a group above. It is of great interest to see traces of this hierarchical arrangement in the facts observed by Mr. Hodson.

The work of some of the etheric forms has been described, and will be fully dealt with in the pages that follow. The higher fairies, sylphs, and salamanders have their centre of consciousness at the astral level, and dip down into the physical plane chiefly to stimulate the life of trees and larger plants. They may live as the ensouling life of a tree or group of trees (like the "dryads" of tradition), the magnetism of their bodies stimulating the far slower activities of the tree, the circulation of sap, etc.; or they may be engaged in raying out strong influences over certain spots, termed "magnetic centres," which have been put under their charge, or in assisting in the building, stabilising and distribution of thought-forms, such as those resulting from the use of religious and magical ceremonies, orchestral music, etc. The still more evolved devas or angels, who have reached the level of self-consciousness, become the guardians of special nations and groups, attached to work of special importance in the scheme of evolution, either on the physical or other planes, and acting as angel messengers who carry out the will of the Most High in all the worlds.

This study of the "life side" of growth may help us to a better understanding of that driving resistless intelligence that we veil under the mass-unity name of "Nature."

The agents distributing her abundant life thus become real and companionable, and, further, we may realise something of our human duty in partnership with them. As we cease to ignore the activities of the devas and nature-spirits, and recognise their partial dependence on human mentality and the amazing response forthcoming when recognition is given, we shall find many of our difficulties and problems solved for us and the world far more wonderful than anything we have yet conceived.

E. L. GARDNER.

January, 1925.

CHAPTER I

THE brownies I have studied, though varying considerably in detail, have always presented certain common characteristics which placed them unmistakably in their own family.

A mediæval style of attire is invariably affected. A short brown coat, sometimes with a wide scalloped collar, bright buttons and facings of green, brown knee breeches, rough stockings, and two distinct kinds of boots: sometimes a large heavy "agricultural" boot is worn; at others a long pointed shoe of lighter make. How variations occur will be seen from the description given later, of the manufacture of a pair of fairy shoes.

A long pointed cap is the usual head dress, though a low-brimmed hard hat occasionally replaces the deer-skin nightcap-shape more generally worn. Groups of brownies, hard at work, have been noticed to be wearing aprons closely resembling those worn by blacksmiths; bright buckles and clasps are generally part of their equipment. Working brownies carry and pretend to use tools, chiefly spades and picks, with which they delve in the earth with great earnestness.

Brownies vary in build: some tribes being short and squat, with fat, round bodies and short limbs; others being slim and youthful in appearance. Their height varies from four inches to a foot. Usually the face is that of an old man, with grey eyebrows, moustache and

beard, red complexion, and a weather-beaten aspect.
The eyes are small and beady, and the expression simple,
kindly and bucolic.

By nature they are communicative and friendly
creatures, living in tribes, and, like most of the fairy
peoples, highly imitative in their habits, their attire, and
their methods of work and play. They belong to the
soil, and have much of the rustic simplicity of the tiller
of the ground. Apparently the type is of mediæval origin;
at any rate, their present appearance is certainly moulded
upon the countryman of that period. What function
they perform in the processes of Nature is not clear;
they are generally to be found on or just beneath the
surface of the ground, and amongst the roots of trees and
plants. I have seen them digging most solemnly amongst
the roots of growing plants, yet such an expression of
mock seriousness and make-believe pervades all their
activities that it is never quite clear whether they
regard their endeavours as work or play. The following
accounts of several different occasions on which they
have been observed may help us to an understanding of
them.

A BROWNIE VILLAGE

*In a thick wood consisting of oak and hazel, with some
beech. Lake District. June 28th, 1922.*

" On the steep side of one of the crags on the western
shores of Thirlmere is a very large colony of brownies;
they live just below the ground level and spend their
time as much beneath as above the surface. I see a
number of tiny little houses, just beneath the surface
of the hill. They are quite perfect in shape, mostly
wooden and thatched, and they have windows and

doors. They are scattered irregularly about the hillside.
In among them, and the roots and rocks which surround
them, numbers of brownie figures are to be seen. The
following is an attempt to describe one selected at
random.

Not more than six inches high, he looks like a little
old man, wearing a brown hat shaped like a nightcap,
and a brown suit, consisting of what appears to be
the brownie regulation knickerbockers, stockings and
boots. The face is grey-bearded, and bears the impress
of an ancient rusticity. Undoubtedly there is the make-
believe of domestic life, though I do not see any female
figure in this fairy village. Brownies literally swarm
over this hillside and vary very little in appearance,
expression, or intelligence. They seem to be just
'evolving' here. They differ from any brownies I have
previously seen in that they do not appear to *work* in
connection with any processes of Nature; though they
venerate the trees, they do not appear to serve them in
any capacity.

One of the more boyish nature-spirits which also 'live'
here has now approached me, and, standing some two
or three yards on my right, is proceeding to 'show off,'
with extravagant gestures and simple-minded humour.
He is much slimmer than the older-looking brownies,
and has a touch of colour about him—a little red on
the hat (which is conical with the point hanging back
slightly) and a little green in his brown costume. I hardly
think he can be a brownie; his feet run down to a point,
his nether limbs are thin and elongated, and his hands
are far too large for the rest of his body. He rests
his left hand on his hip, and points with his right hand
in the direction of the wood, as if proudly displaying the
beauties of the place: added to his pride there is a good

deal of vainglory and childish self-satisfaction. His face is clean shaven and red, his eyes are small, his nose and chin are prominent, his mouth is very wide and still further expanded into a grin. His gestures and poses are amazing. His body is so supple that he can bend and stretch himself to almost any position.

I cannot persuade him to approach any nearer, as he immediately begins to show apprehension. He appears to feel uncomfortable, though not, I think, really afraid. The human ' aura ' is inharmonious to him and he would probably lose his equilibrium within it. By contrast I realise how ethereal and fragile is his make-up, possessing less consistency than a puff of wind; yet the form is perfectly clearly outlined, and the details are sharply defined.

Looking again at the brownie community and striving to grasp some of the details of their life, certain peculiar facts present themselves. For example, an endeavour to see the inside of their houses showed to my surprise that they had no inside—that when one went in at the door there was nothing there! The outside shape is fairly perfect and quite picturesque, but the inside is just darkness. In fact the illusion of a house entirely disappears when the consciousness is directed to the interior. Certain fine lines of flowing magnetism are all that one sees. The brownies enter by the door and then put off the brownie form, and descend deeper into the earth in a relatively formless state. They all seem to have the conception of being busy, hurrying about the place in a pseudo-serious manner—but to me the whole thing is pure make-believe. There does not appear to be much communication between them, and they are all exceedingly self-centred.

The houses do not belong to any individual or group

—any member of the colony uses them, this 'use' being limited merely to passing in and out through the door. They certainly get some satisfaction from contemplating the exterior of these houses. I do not see belonging to these woodland brownies, any of the working tools, satchels, or aprons which I have noticed on other occasions. They appear to be less intelligent and less highly evolved, more self-centred and far more aimless in their existence than any others I have met."

A HOUSEHOLD BROWNIE

Preston, January, 1922.

"For some weeks my wife and I have been aware of the presence of a nature-spirit of the brownie family inside the house. He was first observed in the kitchen on the shelf over the range, and later in the hall and the drawing-room. He differs somewhat in consciousness and appearance from the working brownies whom we have hitherto observed. This evening he entered the drawing-room, *via* the closed door, through which he has been seen to pass and repass. He began gambolling round the room, and the occasional flash of etheric light which accompanied his rapid movements attracted my attention. I gathered from him that these movements were expressive of his pleasure at my return after an absence of three days. He evidently regards himself as a member of the family, while there is also the suggestion that *he has adopted us*. This state of affairs gives him much happiness, and he contrives to give the impression of belonging to the place.

He is some five or six inches high, wears a conical brown cap, of a texture like deerskin, tilted at the back of his head. He has a bright, youthful clean-shaven countenance, with fresh colour, and dark brown eyes which are round and bright. The neck is a little too long and thin for our sense of proportion. He is clothed in a green, close-fitting coatee, knee-breeches, and brownish-grey stockings of a rough material; at the present moment he is wearing large boots somewhat out of proportion to the rest of his body.

He is very lively, very familiar, and evidently has some regard for us, though normally we are not aware of his presence. I gather that the kitchen is his proper habitat, and that in some way the sight of household utensils pleases him. Again, unlike those of his kind that we have hitherto met, he does not belong to a band, and appears to have neither kith nor kin. On my saying this he looked up at me from the sitting posture which he assumed at the time I began to describe him, with an expression which plainly conveyed that as far as he was concerned *we* were his kith and kin.

He finds his amusements and occupation in a manner all his own, and evidently possesses all he needs within himself. In his small way he has idealised the house, the hearth, the household affairs, and appears to gain great satisfaction from his association with them. His intelligence is absurdly childlike; he has no reasoning faculty, and little of what we call the instinct in animals. He just plays and amuses himself with imaginary occu-pations, to pursue which he often retires into a corner and becomes oblivious of everything outside the thought world he creates for himself. To me this appears as a lavender-blue haze of glamour, surrounding him like a large cocoon; therein he plays much as a child plays with its bricks. He knows of our goings and comings; he showed himself clearly on a recent occasion when we were about to leave the house for ten days. Beyond the effect upon him of the human emanations, I see no purpose for his presence. He certainly does not appear likely to fulfil the legends of his type and perform any household duties! Though he does not materialise he is able to increase his visibility and to change his form from that described to a more subtle one."

MANUFACTURE OF FAIRY BOOTS

Facing Helvellyn. November, 1921.

" Among the little folks on this hillside the first observed was an elderly brownie, who, soon after we had seated ourselves, stepped out to the edge of the little firwood behind us.

He was some six or eight inches high and wore a long pointed cap, like a slightly imperfect cone, and a little green jerkin scalloped at the lower edge and falling about his hips; it was edged with brown, fastened with buttons, and had a broad cape-like collar, also scalloped and edged; little trousers completed his attire. At first he showed the lower limbs of an elf (*i.e.*, long and pointed). He had a long, grey, scanty beard, and both his face and body were thinner and more austere than those of the usual brownie. He reminded me slightly of a caricature of Uncle Sam, clothed in the costume attributed to Falstaff.

He took much interest in our dog and approached close to its nose, being absolutely fearless. He appeared unable to take in the group as a whole. He realised the presence of human beings, but the first detail which struck him was the type of boots which I was wearing— canvas-topped army gum-boots. After looking at mine steadily he proceeded to make himself a very respectable imitation of them of which he was inordinately proud. His own simple mental image was sufficient to cover his own feet with a copy of what he looked at so admiringly. After strutting about for a time, as if to get used to them, he finally stalked off into the woods."*

ELVES

My experience of the elf is very limited, and I have only the two brief descriptions given below to offer as examples of a type which does not appear to be very common in those parts of the country I have visited for the purposes of investigation. Elves differ from other nature-spirits chiefly in that they do not appear to be clothed in any reproduction of human attire, and that their bodily constitution appears to consist of one solid mass of gelatinous substance, entirely without interior organisation.

WOOD ELVES

Under the old beeches in the wood at Cottingly. August, 1921.

" Two tiny wood elves came racing over the ground past us as we sat on a fallen tree trunk. Seeing us, they pulled up, about five feet away, and stood regarding us with considerable amusement, but quite without fear. They appeared as if completely covered in a tight-fitting one-piece skin, which shone as if wet, and was coloured like the bark of a tree. There were a large number of these figures racing about the ground. Their hands and feet were large, out of all proportion to the rest of their bodies. Their legs were thin, and their large ears ran upwards to a point, being almost pear-

* Reprinted from *The Herald of the Star*, December, 1922.

shaped. Their noses, too, were pointed and their mouths were wide. No teeth, no structure existed inside the mouth —not even a tongue, so far as could be seen—just as if the whole were made up of a piece of jelly. A small green aura surrounded them. The two we specially noticed lived in the roots of a huge beech tree, and finally disappeared through a crevice, into which they walked as one might walk into a cave, and sank below the ground."

SEASIDE ELVES

Blackpool. July, 1921.

" Playing on the shore, amongst the seaweed and the stones, are queer little elf-like forms. They have large heads, elfish faces, large ears, little round bodies, and short, thin legs ending in a foot which appears almost web-like. They are from three to six inches in height. They are familiar with human beings, and are in no way disturbed by their presence. They do not appear to go into the sea."

CHAPTER II

GNOMES

THE gnome is usually classified as an earth-spirit. Investigation shows that while all the types of traditional fairy actually exist in Nature, there are wide divergences within each type. Some of the differentiations are so great as to call for new names and classifications.

In the future when the naturalist, ethnologist and explorer enter Fairyland, and its scientific text-books are studied in every school, new names will of necessity be given to all the many and various kinds of fairy people. As I find the traditional names to be the most satisfactory from many points of view, I have classified such inhabitants of Fairyland as I have studied under the name given to the race they most nearly resemble.

Examples of tree creatures and winged mannikins are described in this chapter, although they differ in many important particulars from the true gnome. The student may demur at a winged gnome which lives in a tree, nevertheless, so far as my observation goes, the bodies of those I have classed under this heading resemble the gnome more closely than any other type. I shall class as " Gnomes," therefore, several creatures which differ, in many respects, from the true gnome of fairy tradition.

The gnome is usually thin and lanky, grotesque in appearance, cadaverous and lantern-jawed, and is generally, though not always, a solitary. He gives the impression of extreme old age; his whole appearance, bearing, and attire are utterly remote from those of the present day. His arms are too long for our sense of proportion, and, like his legs, are bent at the joints as if they had grown stiff with age. The complexion is very rough and coarse, the eyes are small and black, sloping slightly upwards at the sides. It has been said that the gnome form is a relic of the days of ancient Atlantis, and if this is true it may mean that the type is a representation of the appearance of the peoples of those days, and though grotesque to us, is an expression of their standard of beauty.

The true earth gnome is not a pleasant type of elemental; those met with in England have been either quite black or peat-brown in colour, and though I have never incurred their hostility their atmosphere is decidedly unpleasant.

A Tree Gnome

In the fields near Preston. September, 1921.

" Living in the lower portion of an ash tree is a gnome. He appears larger than any gnome I have ever seen, being, probably, two feet six inches high to the top of his cap. He assumes his gnome shape when preparing to leave the tree, which he does in order to make short excursions into the field. He moves across the field swiftly, at not less than twenty miles an hour, yet, in spite of his speed, he appears to pick his way fantastically over the grass, taking long strides and lifting his legs high into the air. He is in a happy mood, thinking of himself, his tree, and his excursions, while in the background of his mind there are memories of play, mostly of a solitary nature, beneath the branches of the tree. These memories and their complementary anticipations increase his happiness. There does not appear to be the slightest room for anything but joy in his mind. His pleasures are in himself. He does not need the companionship of his kind in order to be happy. His happiness is therefore permanent and stable. He appears to live very largely in the present.

Apparently he has lived for a very long period of time, the passage of which appears to make little or no impression upon him, either mentally or physically. An attempt to contact him whilst he is *inside* the tree produces a curious result in my consciousness: the trunk of the tree becomes transparent, with the gnome in the centre as in a glass case—with this difference, that the material of the surface is continued solidly through the tree; this etheric double of the tree is pale grey with a greenish tinge. The gnome seems to discard his traditional form when inside the tree. The trunk of the tree appears like a cylinder which, without the presence of the gnome, would be of one colour—that of the vital forces of the tree; the presence of the gnome gives individuality to these forces, as they are strongly affected by his rate of vibration.

When the gnome desires to leave the tree, the first phenomenon that I can see is that he slowly assumes the gnome form, thereby encasing himself in denser matter. Having assumed his form he steps out on to the ground, and it is only then that I am really able to contact him as an individual. His features, especially the chin, are long and sharp, the cheek bones are high and prominent, the face thin and rather cadaverous, the eyes elongated like a Chinaman's, the pupils small and beady; the ears are large and protrude above his cap,

and his hair is dark in colour. There is a touch of red
about the cap somewhere, but otherwise he is rather
monochromatic, being of about the general colouring of
the bark of a tree. When he leaves the tree he remains
in magnetic contact with it, and I should say that the
distance he may travel is limited. It is as though the
etheric double of the tree were used to form his body,
so that when he leaves the tree its etheric double stretches.
This is his present condition, but there may be times
when he is completely free. It is very curious to see
him step into the tree, as one would step through a
doorway. He appears always to come out of the tree at
the same place and in the same direction, *i.e.*, on the
south side."

A ROCK GNOME

Lake District. June, 1922.

" Deep within the solid rock behind us there is an
evolving consciousness, which manifests chiefly as formless blotches of colour, a sort of embryo gnome; the
beginnings of the head are visible in shadowy outline,
together with the eyes and mouth, but the rest of the
body is only faintly suggested, like the preliminary work
of an artist, who might put in his main patches of colour
and leave the clear outlines to a later stage. But for this
vagueness the creature would be excessively ugly, not to
say monstrous in appearance. To etheric sight the whole
rock is transparent and the creature appears as if within
a huge glass receptacle, through which it is only vaguely
aware of its surroundings. The only power of volition
that it appears to possess is that of slowly changing
the focus and direction of its dim and limited consciousness; this it does very vaguely and dreamily. The

main colourings, which are of considerable density, are red, green and brown, and these are stirred by faint ripples only, in response to the slowly awakening consciousness.

The presence of this creature gives a certain individuality to the rock, noticeable on the physical plane as a magnetic vibration. It is difficult to judge its size, but it is probably ten to fifteen feet high. The feet that are to be are deep below the surface of the earth in which the rock is buried, and the head some three feet from the top of the rock."

A DOMESTIC GNOME

Lake District. June, 1922.

" While watching other nature-spirits my attention was attracted towards a large rock some forty yards away, beneath which is a gnome who lives under the ground. I caught a glimpse of him as he disappeared under the rock. He was a quaint dark grey figure, diminutively and grotesquely human, and was wearing a hat which rose to a point over his head and then fell over forwards, as if by the weight of a little tassel which hung from the point; the face was that of an old man, thin, cadaverous and lantern-jawed, with a long grey beard. He was clothed in a grey suit, with a coat reaching just below the waist. In his right hand he carried a little light, not unlike a candle, which shone with a yellow gleam.

He descended into the earth, two or three feet below the stone, and moved about without obstruction. He had caught the human idea of a house, and appeared to imagine that the place was his home and that he needed a light. I should say he had observed people going to bed and was imitating them; he was laughably serious in his make-believe. He did not appear to work; he only made occasional journeys down to the water's edge, a distance of about forty yards.

Now, as I watch for him, he has re-appeared with a different kind of head-dress. This time it is an elongated top hat, and, in general effect, he reminds me a little of the picture of the caterpillar which sat on the mushroom in *Alice in Wonderland*. He has the characteristic of curiosity highly developed. He would peep through windows and observe the habits of humans, and, though lacking the mentality to form any judgment from his observations, he would memorise and imitate many of the daily customs of those whom he watched. I see now why I got the idea, when I first saw him, that his cap was a nightcap and he was going to bed; evidently he was doing so for his own amusement, in imitation of human ways, regardless of the fact that he has no need to retire, to put on a nightcap or to take a light, and that he has no bed or bedroom, except the memory of one which lingers in his mind. His powers of concentration failed him as soon as he got below the earth, his manner and even his appearance changed and he reappeared at the surface with a new set of imaginations. This time he was going out—his ideas did not appear to extend beyond that fact—hence, I suppose, the top hat! Immediately after, a vacant look came over his face, his ideas came to an end, and even his form appeared to dissipate for the time being.

A few minutes later he was seen moving swiftly down to the lakeside with a diminutive bucket, which he solemnly dipped in the water and bore, with immense satisfaction, back to his rock. Out he came again immediately, but this time without the bucket, and I saw the little form travelling swiftly, some two feet above the surface, out over the lake—where I lost him. Needless to say the bucket and the water which it was supposed to carry were ' of the stuff that dreams are made of,' the ' water' actually looking like a wisp of grey smoke or mist in the bucket. Life for this little gentleman appears to consist of a continuous series of excursions: each has a special purpose, which is sometimes quite clear, and at other times extremely vague. All he does is imitative of human beings. He certainly has a kind of affection for the rocks, grass and earth, which make up and surround his home."

Dancing Gnomes

In a field near Preston.   September, 1922.

" There are some gnomes here which are at a lower stage of development than the tree-gnomes. They are smaller in size, being about four to six inches high. The gnome photographed a few years ago * probably belongs to this type. They differ from the tree gnome in that they are not solitary, but live and play in groups, their antics and games being weird and grotesque in the extreme. They are gaily coloured little fellows and use much stronger and brighter shades than do the fairies. The group which I am observing is dancing in a half circle; they are holding each other's hands and are swinging from side to side; their legs are not straightened and the knees point outwards. Their arms are too long and not perfectly straight at the elbow. They grin in an odd childlike way, and their beady dark eyes are gleaming with a queer expression as if they were experiencing inward ecstasy. Their wings, shaped

* See *Fairies*, by E. L. Gardner.

like those of the bat, are opened out laterally behind them, and are of a darker colour than their bodies, smooth and furry in substance and of extremely fine texture.

Apparently their contact with each other, their oscillating movement, though purposeless on the physical plane, produces a highly pleasurable astral sensation. I see that it has the effect of disturbing and exciting the astral body, which is just a cloud of unorganised matter about twice the size of the physical. Undoubtedly they are also imposing a special kind of vibratory force upon it.

In repose, or semi-repose, the astral body is an almost shapeless cloud of matter; it is only slightly tinged with colour and has the effect of moonlight. There are shades of red and pink, and of gleaming yellow something like that of an autumn leaf, and also russet browns. When exalted by the dance, from the centre of the astral body (approximately at the solar plexus) vibrations begin, stirring the whole body into life as they sweep through it in waves and ripples. The colours then become more intense, the aura increases, and the gnome is enjoying, to the fulness of his capacity, the effects thus produced.

Suddenly their movement changes, although the original semi-circular formation is maintained. They now dance backwards and forwards, raising and bending their legs and replacing their feet upon the ground in comically fantastic attitudes. They appear only conscious of the brilliant sunshine and the vital condition of the atmosphere.

They have nothing of the flashing rapidity of the fairies, or even of the wood-elves. They are quaint, stiff and antique in their movements. Nevertheless, they have, like all astral and etheric creatures, the power of rapid motion through space."

MOORLAND GNOMES

Wryesdale. Facing an open moorland surrounded by hills. November, 1922.

"Moving about, in the long rough grass and tufts of rushes, are large numbers of gnomes; they present some unusual features.

Their height varies from eighteen inches to two feet six inches; they are male in appearance, and of one colour, which is a very dark brown, rather like peat, of which substance the soil hereabouts largely consists. The face and hands are of the same dark colour. Their hats are long and pointed, with very narrow curled brims; they fit tightly on the head, the point slanting away behind. The features are strongly marked and prominent—the nose, in particular, being long and curved, and having at its extremity a kind of protuberance, of an inch in length. The chin also is prominent and protruding, and the mouth is wide, and set in a perpetual grin. The skin is rough, and of a spongy texture. The eyes are black, beady and elongated. There is the appearance of a close-fitting garment, but it is of the same texture as the skin. This garment begins with a roll at the neck and finishes at the wrists and knees in the same way: calf, ankle, and foot are all in one piece, the foot coming to a point and being eight or nine inches long. They are very loose-limbed and move with long prancing strides, though it is evident that they can also travel through the air with great speed, as I see some moving in this way, just skimming the ground.

An interesting attempt has just been made by one of them to blot out my vision. From his head—I think from the centre of his forehead—issued a widening stream of brilliant grey luminous mist, which impinged upon my aura, and formed a kind of filmy cloud before my face; he continued to pour this out, and, had I been using etheric sight only, he would, I think, have achieved his object. The power of concentration shown is remarkable. He is standing some fifteen yards away, and has succeeded in enveloping our little group with his mist-like projection, which probably has the effect of hiding us from him. It is evident that he objects to us, and that he does not like the close scrutiny and concentrated attention to which he is subjected and which he instinctively resents.

The other members of the species are continually passing to and fro among the grasses; they cannot be said to be playing, though, beyond the fact that they like the sunshine and seem impelled to constant motion, I cannot see any reason for their journeyings.

Here, too, the imitative faculty shows itself, and it is evident that we were observed as we crossed the fields, for I see more than one gnome carrying a basket, resembling, with a fair amount of accuracy, the one in which we brought our food. This gives them pleasure, which is expressed in an almost idiotic grin. They are ludicrous in the extreme as they pace about with their baskets, of which there are now quite a dozen!

They are earth creatures, and the earth is their habitat; I do not think they are able to rise much above their own height into the air. Certainly the earth is not *solid* to them, as some of them are moving with their ankles and feet below the surface, without obstruction. Closer contact with their consciousness shows it to be ultra primitive and very limited. The method by which such creatures progress is not easy to comprehend, for, apparently, Nature offers no resistance to them, and whatever desires they may have seem to be fulfilled. When I endeavour to contact their subterranean existence, they appear to dissolve and in some way to lose their separate individuality, melting into a common essence as they sink below the ground. Globules form in this essence and move about below the earth quite freely and, following one, I see that on rising above the ground it becomes instantaneously a gnome of full size. I cannot see that this metamorphosis is due to any intelligent effort, and am inclined to assume it to be more or less automatic. They seem to know that it will happen, though whether this knowledge is a cause or an effect of the phenomenon I am not able to discover. The tribe is animated almost entirely by group consciousness and herd instinct."

CHAPTER III

MANNIKINS

THIS name has been chosen for all the fairy people of male appearance who cannot be classified as either gnome, brownie, or elf, but who exhibit some of the characteristics of all these, together with certain specific features of their own.

As will be seen from the description given, some nature-spirits may have the face of a gnome, and the clothing of a brownie, perhaps with the long pointed foot of the elf.

Mannikins are to be found in connection with trees, hedges, bracken, grass, heather and wild flowers. Those concerned with trees generally " live " in the trunk and branches, just inside the bark, through which they pass for purposes of recuperation and for work in connection with the growth and colouring of the branches and leaves.

The bracken and grass mannikins are nearly always dressed in green; their faces look like those of young children of about three years old; chubby, and with a happy, smiling expression. A little green cap is nearly always worn, the eyes are bright and beady, and, occasionally, small pointed ears stick up above the cap.

Twice I have come across mannikins who were by no means the pleasant creatures described above. In these the features were prominent, the nose being large and curved and the eyes slanting upwards and narrowed to mere slits, through which the consciousness looked out with an unpleasantly malicious and leering expression.

I have tried to communicate with individual members of the more pleasant sort, but their intelligence is very primitive—much below that of an animal—and I have not had much success.

During instruction in the army we were frequently ordered to " go through the motions " of loading a rifle or machine gun for purposes of practice. The same phrase seems the best one to describe the " speech " of the mannikin. They " go through the motions " of speech; indeed, they sometimes appear to be shouting loudly and extravagantly, but no sound that I have been able to catch issues from their widely-opened mouths. This is very typical of the lower orders of the nature-spirits who imitate many of the ways of Humanity without the slightest understanding of their meaning and purpose.

One little fellow, of whom a description is given later, was proud of the trees in which he lived and worked and he tried to say so; he was quite pleased at being noticed and did his very best to help on the conversation, but his natural limitations stood in his way.

On all occasions when speech has been attempted, or when the little folk have done us the honour to approach us, they have never actually entered the adult human aura, but always remained some distance beyond its direct radiation. If they came nearer, or if a too intense scrutiny was directed upon them, they lost their equilibrium, becoming confused and helpless, finally disappearing, either retiring to a safe distance or into a higher dimension. This, of course, only refers to the little mannikins and not to the very stable gnomes, the more mature brownie, or to the fairy proper.

Certain races of mannikins have small oval wings, of a glistening semi-transparent substance. These are not used for purposes of flight, as far as one can judge, though they tremble and quiver at every movement of their owner.

Observations in different parts of England have led me to the conclusion that the mannikin is the most common fairy type in this country, although many variations are to be seen in different parts. An almost invariable experience has been that, while we were investigating other orders of nature-spirits, numbers of mannikins have approached us. They will stand or sit at a distance varying from eight to twenty feet, in groups and pairs, gazing at us with undisguised curiosity. Examples of this type have been observed in Kensington Gardens.

When they communicate with each other, I am conscious of something closely resembling the twitter of the sparrows, and it has frequently been obvious that our personal characteristics have provided them with an absorbing subject for conversation. As a rule they are quite fearless, neither friendly nor unfriendly, drawing near us entirely from curiosity.

TREE MANNIKINS

A wood near Kendal. December, 1922.

"Connected with the trees are numbers of brownie-like mannikins, pottering about on the surface of the ground, amid the undergrowth and fallen leaves. Their faces are like those of elderly men; their complexion is ruddy, their beards pointed, and their eyebrows are

grey. They have the usual conical cap, but in this case
the point hangs slightly forward. The face is thin, the
features sharp, and in this they differ from the brownie,
as also in their spare forms, thin legs and pointed feet.
A dark russet-brown coatee is worn, which hangs loosely
over the hips, with a short nether garment, and grey,
rough-looking stockings, which run off into a pointed
foot. I do not think they wear boots. They are happy
little fellows, and this is expressed in their faces, which
wear a perpetual smile, as well as in their dark beady
eyes. The eyeballs are glass-like and appear to be all
black or dark brown: I do not see any white. They move
slowly and, as far as I can see, without purpose; occasionally a little group combines in a sort of game. Four such
just appeared on the pathway, joined hands and spun
round clockwise, for about twenty seconds, then, still
holding hands, they floated off further up the woods.
Some of the tribe show an appearance of greater age and
less activity than others.

I saw one very old specimen seated at the foot of an
ash tree, his thin legs stretched out in front of him; he
really looked tired. His coat, which had a wide scalloped
collar, was drawn in slightly at the waist by a belt
that looked like brown leather. As I watched him he
faded into the tree, and I was able to see the process
of disintegration of the form, which appeared to hover
in existence for a fraction of a second after its occupant
had retreated. He did not dissipate it while still wearing
it; he withdrew from it, passing out through the head.
Some impress of this form still remained upon him
while he withdrew, for I distinctly saw the appearance
of two long legs follow him into the tree. Closer
observation showed that the form had not entirely disappeared, the outline of it remained, colour and structure

having gone; in fact it looked just like a fairy ghost, the shape being outlined in grey light, and remaining seated just as it was left. While observing the form I lost touch with the consciousness, which retreated to the centre of the trunk of the tree, and appeared to spread itself out into the corporate cell life of the tree.

(*Ten minutes later*.)

The little man who faded into the tree has come out again, entirely rejuvenated; he is now quite sprightly. While I was describing something else, my attention was attracted to his reappearance by a bright light which appeared at the foot of the tree, and, on being scrutinised, proved to be the same little man, now quite refreshed and most evidently wishing to draw our attention to the fact. He now dances extravagantly towards us, covering about half of the eighteen feet which separates us from the tree, and moving back again, holding his head on one side, and extending his legs gracefully as he moves. He is very proud of himself. The whole fairy atmosphere of the wood is entrancing, and this little fellow beckons as he retreats inviting me to come with him into Fairyland. He waves his right arm in the direction of the wood, as would a host iniviting his guests into an enchanted garden."

TREE MANNIKINS

October, 1922.

"Numbers of little men can be seen to be working at the outside of the leaves and branches of a large beech tree. They occasionally fly to the ground and back again to the tree, as though they were fetching some substance and weaving it into the texture of the smaller

D

branches and leaves. They are perhaps four to six inches high, though they vary, their forms being elastic. They look just like little men. They have a long pointed cap and a little coat with a long collar, so long that it looks like a cape falling over their shoulders, and little knee breeches. Their faces are red, as if from exposure to the weather; the eyes are slanting and of non-human expression.

One of them tries to converse with me; he points to the tree with great pride, as if to say, ' This is our work.' He walks with short steps, and sways, as he walks, from side to side, almost with a swagger. He is very amusing to watch. He shouts up into the tree for no purpose whatever, receiving no answer, so far as I can tell. He gesticulates, in his effort to communicate, and is evidently trying to tell me that all the outside portions of the tree are under the influence and care of himself and his fellows. Occasionally one of these flashes out from the tree, hovers in mid-air, then returns to the tree again. Perhaps they absorb vital essence from the air and give it to the tree? The autumn season, with the change of colour, seems to be an important one, for they are all intensely busy. The colour processes appear to engage most of their attention, though the method eludes me. Even though we could converse by question and answer the little man would prove unable to tell me the *modus operandi*, because it is so obvious to him that he thinks there is nothing to explain; he does not even think of what he is doing—if he did I might catch his thought.

Much that they do on the ground appears to have no purpose at all, being merely imitative, they copy the movements of human beings, without understanding their purpose. The leaves and the branches of the trees are

their home, and upon them the whole of their interest
and energy is concentrated, though they do not confine
themselves altogether to one tree, as I see them 'fly' to
an adjacent tree of the same genus."

RED MANNIKINS

Jeffrey Hill, Longridge, Lancashire. November, 1922.

"The hillside is peopled by a variety of mannikin
which we have not met before. Their main colouring
is red. The shape of the head is most peculiar: it is
very much flattened at the sides, and almost comes to
an edge at the centre of the forehead, nose, and chin;
the eyes are on the side of the head, for there is practically no front surface. The complexion is fair and
fresh, though the eyebrows are dark. The eyes are
long and narrow, the ears large, the nose curved and
very sharp and thin; the lips also are very thin and
slope upwards at the corners; the chin is prominent
and pointed. The clothing is strongly reminiscent of
Elizabethan men's dress, and appears to be quilted and
padded, and to consist of doublet and hose with long
pointed shoes, half red and half green. A very quaint,
pointed, crimson hat is worn, which has either a tassel
or a bell—the latter, I think, as I hear a tinkling sound
all over the field. These figures are from four to six
inches high normally, but they can and do enlarge
themselves to the appearance of human size. This
enlargement is not real; they produce the effect of
large size, but I am conscious that all the time they are
but diminutive creatures, just as one is aware of the
actual size of an object, while seeing it greatly magnified
through a microscope. Hat, clothing and tights are of
bright crimson colour, the upper garment is slashed

over white. This is a very big colony, apparently numbering thousands. They are able to rise into the air, but mostly they trot about over the field. They are a very happy-natured people, communicative, and affectionate towards each other. There is a sense of 'busy-ness' about them, though I am unable to see that they are doing any work. They are very timid and shy, and gather together at a distance when alarmed. The head is more rounded at the back, tapering towards the front. They are merry creatures and play games, as children do, some dancing in rings, some running along the grass together; an atmosphere of joyousness pervades their world. They must have some geometrical sense, for they form clear figures in their games; for example, I see a circle which has a Latin cross within it. They are conscious, I think, that in forming these symbols they are giving expression to some force which flows through them and produces an added sense of happiness and life."

GREEN MANNIKINS

Bowland Forest, Lancashire.   April, 1922.

" The following description is of one of a race of mannikins dwelling at the higher levels of the moors in the forest of Bowland. The general appearance is that of a diminutive boy, six or eight inches high, with large head, rotund body, thin legs and pointed feet; a close-fitting, bright green, long-pointed cap is worn, with the point sticking out horizontally behind. Nothing else which could be called a garment is visible, though the body is covered with a tight-fitting green and brown sheath. The one under observation is quite a serious little fellow, standing in a small clump of heather near by.

The face is round and chubby, mouth small, nose hardly perceptible, eyes round like saucers, with no eyebrows or lashes. The ears, if any, must be hidden by the cap, which, as I watch it, becomes ringed with circular bands of pink and blue. An etheric emanation is visible all round him, to a distance of about an inch and a half; it is blue-grey in colour and is of much smoother and finer vibration than that of the human kingdom. There is one vital centre, at a point corresponding to the solar plexus, from which these emanations proceed. A small *chakram,** yellow in colour, is working at the top of the head. One might hazard the guess that the form is vivified through the solar plexus, while consciousness functions through the *chakram* in the head. From the centre of this head *chakram* a thin, threadlike connection rises into the air and passes beyond my vision.

This little fellow has seated himself, with an air of patient good-will, and I now see that the ears are small, and pointed at the top; meanwhile his fellows are running, jumping, and flying about, some little distance away. I would not say for certain that they speak, but their interchange of thought, such as it is, seems to reach me in the form of a ceaseless chatter. They are full of life and happiness; and are completely oblivious of everything except themselves and their familiar natural surroundings."

DANCING MANNIKIN

In our Drawing-room, Preston. September, 1922.

"A mannikin is dancing up and down the carpet. He is keeping time to the rhythmical beat of fairy

* A Sanskrit term meaning a wheel and used to denote a whirling centre of force.

music, which appears to consist of two notes continually repeated.

This dancing mannikin has a serio-comic childlike face, a pointed cap, with the point at the back, a coatee and tights, continued into pointed toes. The tights are green, the coatee dark brown, edged with fur or gossamer, there is a tassel on the cap which hangs down behind. He is in an abnormal condition, as though keyed up by surplus energy and extra vitality. His complexion is that of a healthy, outdoor child, his eyes dark brown, large and wondering; he walks with a slight swagger, the body swaying from side to side, his hands are on his hips when he is not gesticulating. He dances several steps, some of which are not unlike a Scotch reel, though he does not pirouette. Two other similar figures are in the room. They are not unlike wood-elves, but their ears are normal and their expression is less weird and more human. These figures are all of male appearance, like little boys of eight or nine. They slide up and down the architrave of the door, they walk on the edge of the back of the settee, they do gymnastics on the bars of the chairs and table. In all of them the colour green predominates, though brown is intermixed with it. They appear to be enjoying themselves hugely. Their natural element seems to be the grass of the fields. They are performing what looks like a test match of long jump on the sofa. This tribe is composed of larger numbers than the groups or parties of brownies. They can move through the air at will. They have small transparent wings, almost oval in shape. Their antics have an air of unreality and make-believe. Their movements are very rapid and it is almost impossible to isolate an individual and study him, with the exception of the first one described, who is larger than the others. I should place him at six inches and the others at four. Some are sliding down the curtains. One of the party now stands in the very centre of the room, gazing up at me. I catch glimpses of others on the picture rails and frames. The standing figure is trying to communicate, and does so by what looks like a tremendous effort of shouting: no sound whatever reaches me. They are not ungraceful figures, having their tunic drawn in at the waist and falling loosely over the hips. Their wings appear to be continually quivering. Their little caps are close fitting round the head, no hair is visible. They have no interior structure, their bodies being all of a piece."

GRASS CREATURES AT HOME

In a glade a few miles from Preston. September, 1921.

" Diminutive green elf-like forms, probably about an inch or two high, with wings of peculiar shape and irregular outline, are to be seen on the ground. Their faces are flesh-like and their whole bodies clothed in a tight-fitting garment of green. They walk about in the grass, and appear to be wholly absorbed in the task of exploring the fairy pathways of what, to them, is a mighty jungle.

Their existence seems to be connected with grass, whose growth is in some way intimately associated with theirs. They move very slowly in and out among the stems; they can fly, although I only see them covering short distances at a time, in rather a clumsy fashion. When in the air their little feet are pointed downwards and forwards towards the place on which they are to land, as if from a trapeze. Their flight, in fact, appears to be more of a swing than anything else. They are very numerous in this field. They make a curious chattering sound as they move about. They are carrying on a single line of thought, which completely occupies their mind; this shows itself in their aura, which is practically colourless, as a succession of tiny globules of light steadily issuing from the head; these thought-forms are all exactly the same, and are connected by a thread of light. They look like tiny bubbles, perhaps a sixteenth of an inch in diameter. Closer contact leads me to think that these elves are talking to themselves all the time, this talk consisting of a constant repetition. Their aura causes the etheric double of the grass to vibrate a little more quickly as they pass through it."

Mannikin compared with Brownie

At Whitendale. April, 1922.

"Whilst this was being written a gruff and rather cross old brownie came out of a clump of rushes near by and passed down the hill towards the mannikins. He was much like the brownies previously described, with slight differences of colour and detail in his dress. He had rather an ugly rough face, stubbly grey beard, and unusually large hands. He was constantly repeating something to himself as he came, probably some decision recently reached, and in the process of being put into execution. The contrast in age of both type and individual is very noticeable when he approaches the little mannikins which are playing about here. His body is rough, rather coarse and heavy in texture, and much less responsive to the impulses of consciousness than that of the mannikins, who appear to be a newer type of nature-spirits. The centre of consciousness in both types is in the head, and is represented by a small *chakram* * which, in the case of the brownie, has retreated a distance of half an inch into the head. Though the personality of the brownie is stronger and more evolved, yet his *chakram* is not so vivid in its life, nor so responsive in its working, as that of the mannikin. The type is becoming very set from age. It is not easy to see, with the limitations of human outlook, how the brownie will progress on to the next stage in its evolution, as both form and consciousness appear so fixed in their present attributes as to preclude their developing any others. Probably external assistance of a forceful nature will need to be given."

* Refer to note on p. 53.

CHAPTER IV

UNDINES AND SEA SPIRITS

THE undine belongs to the element of water and, so far as my experience goes, is never to be found away from river, stream and fall. She is definitely female in form and is always nude; she does not usually have wings, and only rarely wears any kind of adornment. Her form, whether diminutive or of human stature, is always entrancingly beautiful, and all her movements are perfect. The waterfall is her favourite haunt, and there she is to be seen disporting herself, generally with a group of her sisters, enjoying to the full the magnetic force of the fall.

Apparently there are periods when the undine retires from the vivid external life in which she is most frequently observed and finds a measure of quiet and repose deep down in the still cool depths of the pools below the falls or in the quieter reaches of the rivers, as well as in lakes and ponds. This life below the waters is in strong and marked contrast to the amazing vividness and joy she manifests amid falling water and sunlit spray.

The three fundamental processes of Nature—absorption, assimilation and discharge—are expressed fully in the outer life of the undine, indeed that life may be said to consist entirely of a continued repetition of those three processes.

Poised amid the spray, or in the centre of the downward rushing torrent, she absorbs, slowly, the magnetism from the sunlight and the fall; as the limit of absorption is reached, she releases, in one dazzling flash of light and colour, the energy with which she is surcharged. At that magical moment of release she experiences an ecstasy and exaltation beyond anything possible to mere mortals dwelling in the prison of the flesh. The expression on the face and particularly in the eyes at that moment is beautiful, I would almost say wonderful, beyond description. The eyes flash with dazzling radiance, the face expresses rapturous joy and a sense of abnormal vitality and power; the whole bearing, the perfect form, and the brilliant splendour of the auric radiance, combine to produce a vision of enchanting loveliness.

This condition is immediately followed by one of dreamy pleasure in which the consciousness is largely withdrawn from the physical plane and centred in emotion. The form becomes vague and indistinct for the time being, until, having assimilated the whole experience, she reappears and repeats the process.

There are, doubtless, many other kinds of nature-spirits connected with water, and a description of one type, differing from the undine, is included in this chapter.

UNDINES

Whitendale. April, 1922.

" Seated in a heather-covered bower beside a water-fall which flows between two huge stones and falls a distance of five or six feet on to the moss-covered rocks below, an attempt is made to study water-fairies, which are not easy to contact immediately after the consciousness has been attuned to the land-fairies.

They are certainly more subtle and quicker in their movements. They also change their form with bewildering rapidity. As I see them they are like diminutive human females, entirely nude, probably four to five inches tall; their long hair streams behind them and they wear some decoration, resembling a garland of small flowers, round their foreheads. They play in and out of the fall, flashing through it from different directions and calling all the time in wild tones that rise occasionally to what is almost a shriek. This calling is infinitely remote, and reaches me but faintly, like a shepherd's call across some Alpine valley. It is a vowel sound, but as yet I cannot name the series of vowels of which it is composed.

They can travel up the fall against the stream or remain motionless within it, but they generally play and flash through it. When a cloud has passed away from the face of the sun and the fall again becomes brilliantly sunlit, they appear to experience an added joy; they then increase the activity of their movements and their singing. I can nearly represent the sound by the vowels e, o, u, a, i, in one word, which ends with a plaintive and appealing cadence.

There are between eight and twelve of them playing at the fall; some are rather larger than others, the tallest being about eight inches high. One of the tall ones has just increased her size to probably two feet; and now she flashes off, higher up the stream, with great speed. Some of them have rosy-coloured auras and some pale green, and the closer contact, which I am now obtaining with them, shows me what extremely beautiful creatures they are, and at the same time how utterly remote from the human family. They pass in and out of the great rocks at the side of the fall without experiencing any obstruction whatever. I am quite unable to attract their attention or to influence them in any way. Some of them pass under the water in the basin at the foot of the fall, and occasionally appear amidst the swirling froth.

The garland, referred to previously, is luminous, and apparently forms part of their aura."

UNDINES

Thirlmere. By the side of Dab Ghyll. November, 1921.

"There are two different grades of water-spirits at this fall. One is apparently connected with the whole ghyll, and was first seen travelling swiftly up the mountain on which the stream rises. It is definitely of the undine variety, but rather larger than those previously seen, though similar to them in other characteristics.

The figure, which shines as if wet, is female, nude and without wings, the exquisite limbs gleam through the white auric flow, the arms are particularly long and beautiful, and she waves them gracefully in her flight. She is about four feet in height and her general colouring is silvery white, with gold stars round the head.

She moves up the fall by a series of darting motions of exceeding swiftness, disappears from view as if into the rock, reappears, and flashes down again. As I watch her rapid movements she appears suddenly to become languid; her form slowly dissipates and her consciousness sinks into the ground, as if to rest. At the particular place where she disappeared—a large rocky bluff covered with bracken and heather—I can still sense, I would almost say see, the undine, at a distance of six to ten feet below the surface of the ground.

She has reappeared, and obviously experiences considerable joy, taking great interest and delight in the large fall, over which she hovers in a fashion that suggests some emotion akin to brooding tenderness. She shows a certain natural seriousness; in her there is none of that careless inconsequence which marks so many of the lesser nature-spirits. In her mind there is a sense of responsibility for certain aspects and processes of evolution which are taking place here, connected chiefly with the water and the vegetation. Over the rock under which she retired there is a decided magnetic influence, due no doubt to her long-continued presence there, which has given the place a strongly defined aura and influence of its own.

There are some less evolved undines at the actual falls, where they appear to be permanently stationed. They, too, can pass in and out of the rock at will. They differ from the one described chiefly in size; they are less than a foot high, and appear to be making vocal sounds. Their joy is more unrestrained and their whole bearing more irresponsible than hers. They are five or six in number. Their slim, graceful, nude bodies are supple in the extreme, and they constantly assume poses of great beauty as they float in the midst of the fall, or hover just in the edge of the spray. A characteristic attitude is one with the body upright and more or less stiff, limbs straight, arms close to the side, head thrown slightly back, eyes looking upward. In this pose they ride slowly upwards through the falls to the top, like a bubble rising through water; having reached the summit they flash free into the air, releasing the concentrated energy which they appear to have absorbed, making a brilliant display of colour and light, radiating joy and delight in all directions.

They are singing in a high-pitched but full-toned voice, which reaches me as a series of broad vowel-sounds, generally on the ascending scale, and ending on a note almost incredibly high. Just now the sun is full on the falls, and they are making the most of the magnetic vitality which results. This vitality they draw within themselves, until they are charged almost to bursting point. They use quite a strong effort to compress and contain this vital energy, until at last it becomes too much for them and bursts forth in the manner described, impinging visibly on the surrounding rocks, bracken and trees. This process fills the undines with an intense joy; they thrill inwardly during the process of absorption and compression, and at the time of discharge a delirious pleasure is felt. One might almost say that they lose their heads; their actual form becomes indefinite for a moment or two, during which they appear as flashing radiant light. It was, in fact, these flashes of intense brightness which first attracted my attention and led me to try to study them.

Undoubtedly, all this means growth for them and for the scenery amongst which they live. I think the smaller ones are in some measure under the control of the larger nature-spirit first described; certainly she hovered, watching them, during the visit she paid up the stream, when I first saw her."

THE SPIRIT OF THE FALL

Lake District. June, 1922.

" We are in a bower of bracken and rocks, a veritable Fairyland. The spirit of the falls occasionally appears in the form of a full-sized, nude female of singular beauty. She differs in some characteristics from undines previously observed; she is very much larger than those we have seen before, has a more highly developed intelligence, *and is winged.* She seems to ensoul the rocks, trees, ferns and mosses, as well as the actual waterfall itself. When first seen, she sprang out of the solid rock—a marvellously beautiful figure—hung poised for a moment in the air and then disappeared. She repeated this process several times, but whether she is visible or not, her presence can always be most distinctly felt.

Her form is a beautiful, pale, rose pink, and suggests a marble statue come to life. The hair is fair and shining, the brow broad, the features beautifully modelled, the eyes large and luminous, and, while their expression has something of the spirit of the wilds, their glance is not unkindly. The wings, which appear to rise from the shoulder blades, are small in proportion to the body, and would surely be inadequate for flight if such had been their purpose; they, too, are of a rosy pink. Even more striking than the form is the rainbow-like aureole which surrounds her, as a halo surrounds the moon. This aura is almost spherical in shape, and consists of evenly arranged, concentric bands of soft yet glorious hues. The colours are too numerous, and in far too rapid movement, for me to detail them, but her aura would seem to contain all the colours of the spectrum in their palest shades, with perhaps rose, green and blue predominating. Some of the bands of colour are outlined with a golden fire and beyond the outer edge a shimmering radiance of pearly white gives an added beauty. Over the head a powerful upward flow of force interpenetrates the aura in a fan-shaped radiation. This appears to come from a point in the middle of the head, where there is a brilliant golden centre, slightly below the level of the eyes, and midway between them. To contact such a creature is an illumination, and I wish that I could find words to describe not only the splendour of her appearance, but the wonderful feeling of exaltation and life incarnate that she gives. The place is vibrant with her life.

(*A little later.*)

She now reappears: this time she is wearing a jewelled belt, the ends of which cross and hang down on the left side. The jewels are not like any known to us, being large and of fiery luminosity, and the belt is made of something that shimmers like golden chain-mail of extremely fine texture."

LAKE SPIRITS

Wythburn. June, 1922.

" At different parts of the surface of Lake Thirlmere, which lies spread out beneath us, numbers of nature-spirits are to be seen, skimming swiftly over the surface, generally at a height of some six or eight feet, but sometimes rising much higher. Although they usually remain over the water they make occasional flights to the fields.

They resemble large white birds, flying at great speed, and, at this distance, I cannot make out any distinct shape; they take and lose many different forms, with great rapidity: there is a general suggestion of wing-like formation and occasionally the likeness of a human face and head. Again this appearance is lost, and they appear like wisps of white cloud. The swiftness of movement, and the rapidity with which

E

they change their appearance, make it difficult to study them with any degree of accuracy. Perhaps the nearest description of them would be that of fairy auras without a central body: at the same time there is some quite definite organisation within these auras; certain lines, along which the forces flow—consisting chiefly of whirls, vortices and wing-like streamers. Their movement is not unlike that of swallows flying over the surface of a river. They do not appear to enter the water, though they occasionally alight on the shore, shooting up again with a brilliant flash of light. Their colouring is chiefly white, deepening to dove-grey.

They are non-individualised expressions of group consciousness. As I watch, numbers of them have been drawn together into one form (I use the word ' form ' for want of a better term, but the form referred to is the merest film), an envelope of large size, in which they are enclosed as are birds in an aviary. The actual geographical position of this envelope is some distance down the lake, over which it floats like an indefinite balloon of enormous but varying dimensions. In its centre there are a number of very bright points of golden light, which appear as if suspended at different levels. These nature-spirits as they enter the envelope appear to lose their outline, and all that remains is a sense of movement inside it. Next moment they are all let forth again like a flock of doves, to resume their rapid flight up and down the lake."

SEA SPIRITS

N.W. Coast. January, 1923.

Far out at sea are huge, sea-green etheric monsters, fish-like, and yet unlike any fish. Their forms are transparent like glass—shining with a weird green light of their own. They appear to carry themselves upright, and, though they have a head and body, I cannot discern in these creatures any resemblance to the human shape. From the shoulders downwards no limbs appear, the denser form runs almost to a point, and then spreads out into the finer matter of the aura. They seem to rise slowly up from the depths of the sea, sometimes completely out of the water, sometimes only partially so.

Other more airy forms, of a human shape, scud about over the surface of the sea. Amongst them are smaller sea-fairies, riding on the waves and rejoicing in the electric vitality borne in with the incoming tide. By contrast the huge deep-sea creatures are exceedingly slow and heavy of movement, they gaze vacantly around them, their intelligence being very limited and obtuse. There is almost a quality of fierceness in the exultation and joy of the sea creatures, as if they took on something of the power of the sea itself. They are much more active and virile than land-fairies. The smaller ones appear completely concentrated in their own activities.

Far in the distance a group of great sea-devas is visible. The head of each is crowned. They are huge, solemn, majestic rulers of the sea, faintly reminiscent in appearance of the god Neptune.

In the ocean shallows there are sea-nymphs, in shape just like a human woman and of radiant beauty. They are not winged like the land-fairies. They live in colonies both under and on the surface of the sea which is their home. Riding on its waves and sometimes sinking into its depths, they pass a joyous existence. I see them calling to each other in loud voices, crying in exultation as the life forces, of which they are composed, arouse in them an almost unimagined joy. These, as well as the smaller sea-fairies, are much more keenly alive, much more strenuous in their existence than their land brethren.

Far down, in the ultimate depths of the sea, I see huge, filamentoid, vegetable-like, etheric forms, with little or no external consciousness, drifting about with the currents. I can trace the gradual development of form, from the shadowy film-like creature with consciousness wholly inturned, up to the magnificently organised form of the sea-nymph and sea-fairy rejoicing in amongst the breakers. These last are definite and permanently embodied entities. They leap into vision and out again, with the speed of light, and one gets the impression of colour, a hint of form, and they are gone to reappear elsewhere.

The chief difference between the hosts of nature-spirits to be seen over and in the sea appears to be that of size. The majority are human in shape, though there are others more nearly resembling fishes: of the human-shaped varieties, while all are a-sexual, the general appearance is female. A prominent characteristic also is the rapidity with which they take and lose their forms; they constantly change into brilliant and relatively formless flashes of light, and back again into the human form, which appears to be their natural one.

The general rule seems to be that the larger varieties are further out at sea, while the small ones play in and out amongst the breakers. An average size, at a distance of 200 yards out, is a little below the human.

One of the larger variety recently came within a few

yards of us, and I observed that several others flashed short distances inland and back again. The one which came near to us was almost dead white in colour, its body glistening all over as if wet; it was entirely nude, and its form was curiously unstable, so that the difference between the (relatively) dense form and its auric emanations was frequently lost.

Many of them appear to pass their whole time in flashing swiftly over the surface of the sea, now diving, feet foremost, wholly or partially into the water, now shooting, with the swiftness of light, high into the air. They are in a state of exultant joy, bathing themselves in the powerful magnetism of the sea. They absorb some of this magnetic force into themselves and, after a pause, in which some form of assimilation takes place, they discharge it. Their existence is vivid in the extreme, far beyond anything possible to us who live in the dense physical form—even at our periods of highest exaltation.

Further observation appears to support the idea that they continually absorb and discharge force in some form or other. At last I have caught a glimpse of a sea-fairy when, for a fraction of a second, it was relatively motionless; this is a very rare occurrence! It appeared fully charged with vital force, which radiated to a distance considerably beyond that of its normal emanation, say six feet in all directions, giving it the appearance of a glorified and radiantly happy human being, with blazing eyes, standing with arms outstretched in a shimmering aureole of white light. The creature was obviously rejoicing with extreme delight in the sensation of being supercharged with vitality; when this was discharged, and the sensation past, it proceeded to repeat the process.

The smaller varieties of sea-fairies bear some resemblance to the land-fairies that have been photographed,* except that they have no wings and are nude. There also appears to be more variation in size, as the sea creatures in the breakers vary from nine inches to two feet approximately. Contact with them gives rise to quite different feelings. The land-fairy is wholly pleasant and friendly, and its vibrations are harmonious to the human; the sea-fairies, on the contrary, are not as yet within easy reach of consciousness, so far as I am concerned, and their rate of vibration does not readily harmonise with mine. They are also much more self-centred, not appearing to hold much, if any, communication among themselves. There is a good deal of calling, but nothing in the nature of response; indeed, their state of constant and intense activity would appear to render them unreceptive to external communication. (This statement must be taken very generally, as it is obvious that there is some form of group consciousness and communication amongst them.) The smaller varieties do not rise so high in the air as their larger brethren, but they make graceful flights, rarely rising more than thirty or forty feet, more frequently skimming over the surface or riding on the crest of the waves. Those further out at sea rise to great heights, in fact beyond my range of vision.

Watching the Incoming Tide

April, 1922.

As on former occasions I am impressed by the fact that, so far as the eye can see up the coast line and out to sea, the aerial spaces are densely populated with

* See *Fairies*, by E. L. Gardner.

countless numbers of sea-spirits, at various levels of evolutionary progress, from the smaller, human-shaped beings, rejoicing among the breakers, through the orders of large sea-spirits (some of whom appear to resemble fishes, and even birds, though usually with human heads and shoulders), up to the large sea-devas, majestically calm, at their stations far out at sea.

As previously stated, it appears that as the electric vitality of the flowing tide increases, the hosts of sea-spirits clothe themselves in etheric matter in order to participate more vividly in the marvellously refreshing and vitalising magnetism which is created and released as the tide rises higher and higher. When this condition is changed to the comparative quietness of low water, they retire to the astral plane, where they dwell upon the stimulating joys through which they have passed, and await eagerly the turn of the tide, when they can once more repeat these vivid experiences, of which, for them, life seems so largely to consist. It is possible to reproduce within oneself a little of their thrilling ecstasy, by watching them and endeavouring to unite one's consciousness with theirs.

This process of self-exaltation, which they continually repeat, appears to begin some distance out at sea, whence they rush, with inconceivable rapidity, towards the breaker line where they enter the tidal magnetism, which is discharged upwards and forwards during the whole period of flow, increasing in intensity and power as high-water mark is reached.

Entering the magnetic field they become visible in human shape, frequently catching the physical eye with brilliant flashes of white light; then they move forward slowly, absorbing the magnetism and experiencing a sensation of extreme delight, until they reach a stage where even their ethereal organism can contain no more: there is a moment's pause, the face assumes an expression of the most radiant joy and vivid vitality and the whole being is surrounded by an aureole of light, something like an electric discharge; as saturation point is reached the whole force is dissipated; the creature then fades out of etheric vision in a state of dreamy inaction, and retires once more to the astral plane.

During this process the astral body swells to quite twice its normal size (about double that of the dense body); it is enormously quickened by the experience, the effect of which seems to last some considerable time. The force absorbed and discharged becomes impressed with the vibrations of the sea-spirit, which has specialised it, in a similar manner to that in which *prana* is absorbed and specialised by man.

Another variety of sea-spirit is one resembling a huge seagull with a human head, the long white streaming wings being formed by the auric configuration; they are not set quite in the same way as those of the bird, they rather suggest two curved spokes of a wheel and remind me of that familiar agricultural implement, the chaff-cutter, with its big wheel and curved blades. These sea-spirits appear to move not by the ordinary progression of flight, but by turning themselves over and over, wheeling and whirling swiftly through the air, forty or fifty feet above the breakers. Apparently they flash about continuously, without pause, rejoicing, but in a less concentrated and systematic way than those previously described. An average size is about twice that of the large seagull. They look very much like flying white wheels revolving in swift motion through the air.

As I have been describing this, seated on the pier some

thirty or forty feet above the waves, several of the white sea-spirits of human shape have observed us; some of them pulled up suddenly, pausing for a second and looking, with a somewhat startled air, in our direction, as if surprised at seeing a human being attempting to penetrate their kingdom. Their faces are singularly beautiful, and quite human in appearance; even the eyes have not that non-human expression which is so characteristic of all types of nature-devas. It is difficult to say just where the difference between us lies. With us intensity of emotion seems to suggest heat or, at any rate, warmth of feeling; with the sea-spirits I feel an intense coldness, like a vibration from another world, a world physically cold, yet emotionally alive. They remind me of the moon, for, deep within, in spite of all their rapidity of movement and intensity of feeling, there is a cold impassiveness, as if there were no heart beating in this almost mechanical representation of one of Nature's forces. They seem to become more arctic in feeling as their exaltation increases, as if they were just electric magnetism incarnate. The centre of consciousness appears to be in the head, where it shows as a brightly burning flame. They have no permanent etheric body, but are able to assume a temporary one for purposes of contact with the physical plane.

CHAPTER V

FAIRIES

OF all the many denizens of Fairyland that I have seen the true "fairy," as described in this chapter, is the one which it gives me the greatest joy to contact and with which I feel the closest affinity. In order to help the reader to visualise clearly the appearance of a fairy I recommend the study of the fairy photographs in Sir Arthur Conan Doyle's book *The Coming of the Fairies.** I am personally convinced of the *bona fides* of the two girls who took these photographs. I spent some weeks with them and their family, and became assured of the genuineness of their clairvoyance, of the presence of fairies, exactly like those photographed, in the glen at Cottingly, and of the complete honesty of all parties concerned.

A GOLDEN FAIRY
In the Garden. October 17th, 1921.
She is decidedly fair in colouring, full of laughter and happiness, very open and fearless in expression, and is surrounded by an aura of golden radiance in which the outline of her wings can be traced. There is also a hint of mockery in her attitude and expression, as of one who is enjoying a joke against the poor mortals who are studying her.

* The photographs are also published separately by the Theosophical Publishing House, Ltd., 68, Great Russell Street, London, W.C.1.

Suddenly her manner changes and she becomes serious. Stretching out her arms to their full length, she performs an act of concentration which has the effect of reducing the size of her aura and of turning its energies inwards upon herself. Having maintained this condition for about fifteen seconds she releases the whole of the concentrated energy, which pours forth in all directions in streams of golden force, and appears to affect every single stem and flower within its reach. (She is in the centre of a clump of chrysanthemums.) She thus reinforces the vibration which is already there, probably as a result of previous similar activities on her part. Another effect of this operation has been to cause the astral double of the whole clump to shine with an added radiance, an effect which is noticeable right down to the roots.

Manx Fairies

On the western slopes of Snaefell. August, 1922.

We encountered a charming race of " little folk " whilst climbing the mountain from Sulby Glen, a race differing from the English nature-spirits in many respects. In height from four to six inches, they suggest, in miniature, the appearance of men and women of very ancient times. Unlike their brethren of the mainland, they move sedately and with an almost languorous grace about the hillside. Their eyes, which are soft and dreamy in expression, are elongated and narrow. Their faces wear a perpetual smile; the features are well modelled though the chin recedes unduly. Both sexes appear to be represented, the females have long dresses of bright mixed colours; the males are clothed in shiny material that looks like silk, the favourite colour being a royal blue of electric brilliance. They suggest remotely the cavalier and fine lady of the Stuart period, but I imagine that their appearance is modelled upon that of the people of a far earlier date. They make a sweet flute-like music which, coming from several directions at once, creates a kind of twittering effect. They are dancing and playing on the hillside, which they people in countless numbers.

Appearing amongst them occasionally is a creature partly resembling a gnome, but with an animal's hind legs. These little folks have no wings, and lack the vivid vitality which has characterised all the other types of fairies we have met. Their consciousness is only operating very partially through the forms; some of them seem almost to be walking in their sleep. They are extremely gentle and courteous in their relationship with each other, and express love rather than joy. Theirs is a very peaceful, quiet, dreamlike existence.

The centre of vitality appears to be just within the small of the back, the astral body being connected to the physical at that point and floating immediately behind and above it. It is shapeless, and the predominating colours are silver and rose, brilliantly illuminated. The creature appears to be less than half incarnated. Probably the race is so ancient that it is about to die out.

FAIRIES
Kendal, December, 1922.

A very lovely variety of fairy lives here. They have the softest and gentlest expression of countenance that I have yet seen, except perhaps on the faces of the Atlantean fairies seen on the western slopes of Snaefell. These are truly beautiful, and move about in the gentlest, quietest manner, with extreme grace and beauty. One of them has observed us and does not seem to be afraid. She is holding her light filmy garment, through which the pink and white form is just discernible, up with her right hand, and in her left she carries some object, which for the moment I cannot describe; the limbs are bare, the hair is long and hangs loose, tiny lights play like a garland round her head, and so beautiful is her carriage, that, were it not for the complete absence of self-consciousness and the perfect candour shown in the expression of face and eyes, I should have thought she was posing. All around me I see others equally beautiful, each differing in some slight degree from the other. One, whose back is turned towards me, has lovely long dark hair, which hangs down well below the waist; one beautiful white arm is stretched out before her, a little to one side, as she walks slowly through the wood. This place is Fairyland indeed, and would time permit hours could be spent describing the life here.

Preston, 1922.

A beautiful female nature-spirit, exactly like a small tree-deva, has a residence in a thick hedge near by where the growth of brambles, creepers and bright red hawthorn berries is profuse. Evidently processes similar to those in trees take place in big hedges. This nature-spirit is of a particularly engaging character. She is perhaps three or four feet high, lightly robed in a flowing transparent filmy garment, and looks straight at us, with the frankest and friendliest of smiles; she is remarkably vital and gives the impression of great dynamic energy held in perfect control. Her aura is noticeably alive, and looks like a cloud, of soft but radiant hues, through which shafts of dazzling light flash and radiate. The colours are far beyond any earthly colours in delicacy, ranging through shades of soft luminous pale rose, pale soft green, lavender and misty blue, throughout which brilliant lances of light are constantly passing. She is in a state of exalted happiness.

As an experiment I yielded voluntarily to the powerful glamour of her presence, and for a time, unconscious of the body yet always sufficiently awake in it to return at will, experienced some measure of the joyful and radiant happiness which seems to be the permanent condition of all the dwellers in the fairy world. There is danger in too close a contact; it requires a decided effort to withdraw and take up the burden of fleshly existence once again.

(September 26th, 1921. In a glade a few miles from home. Beautiful old trees, touched with autumn tints, a stream gently flowing, and the whole bathed in autumn sunshine.)

The surface of this field is densely populated by fairies, brownies, elves and a species of grass creature, something between an elf and a brownie, but smaller, and apparently less evolved than either.

The fairies are flitting through the air in short flights, taking very graceful poses as they fly. They express in the highest degree the qualities of light-heartedness, gaiety and *joie de vivre*. A number of them are flying about singly. They flit from place to place, pausing a moment between each flight. They seem to be bearing something which they give to the grass or the flowers at each stopping place, at least they put out their hand and touch the place where they come to rest, as if applying some substance, then they move swiftly away again.

They become more clearly visible as they alight and as they move away; one loses them after have landed. They are female, dressed in a white, or very pale pink, clinging, sheeny material of exceedingly fine texture. It is drawn in at the waist and shines with many colours like mother-of-pearl. The limbs are uncovered, the wings are oval, small and elongated.

DANCING FAIRIES

Cottingly. August, 1921.

A bright radiance shines out over the field, visible to us sixty yards away. It is due to the arrival of a group of fairies. They are under the control of a superior fairy who is very autocratic and definite in her orders, holding unquestioned command. They spread themselves out into a gradually widening circle around her and, as they do so, a soft glow shines over the grass. Since two minutes ago, when they swung high over the tree tops and down into the field, the circle has spread to approximately twelve feet in width and is wonderfully radiant with light. Each member of this fairy band is connected to the directing fairy, who is in the centre and slightly above them, by a stream of light. These streams are of different shades of yellow deepening to orange, they meet in the centre merging in her aura, and there is a constant flow backwards and forwards along them. The form produced by this is something like an inverted fruit dish with the central fairy as the stem, and the lines of light, which flow in a graceful even curve, forming the sides of the bowl.

Their continued activities were producing an ever-increasing complexity of form, when time, unhappily, forced us to depart.

A group of fairies are gambolling and dancing on a little plateau on the other side of the stream. Their bodies are female, their main clothing is pale blue; their wings, which are almost oval in shape, are constantly fluttering as they dance in a ring hand in hand. Some of them wear a loose girdle, from which is suspended an instrument like a horn. All are draped with a material which serves to conceal the form more completely than is usual with this type of nature-spirit. Their height is probably six inches. Their hair, which in all cases is brown, varies from very light to quite dark shades.

The colouring of the fairy form is a very pale rose pink, beyond which, in nearly all cases, is a pale blue aura and pale blue wings.

They are performing something not unlike a country dance; and I think it must be their thought that produces numbers of tiny daisy-like flowers, which appear and disappear—coming sometimes as single flowers and sometimes as wreaths or chains.

They are discharging into the surrounding atmosphere a good deal of specialised energy, in the form of silver sparks, and the effect produced by this miniature electrical display, flowing through their auras and through the curious misty glamour, or haze, in which the whole group is bathed, is most beautiful; it extends to a height of probably eight or ten inches over their heads, and reaches its highest point over the centre of the group. The effect of it upon the fairies is to give them the sense of complete seclusion: in fact, the nature-spirits of other species which are in the neighbourhood do not enter within the charmed sphere.

They have now changed their formation and are going through an evolution of considerable intricacy, making radial chains across the circle. They do not remain in exactly the same spot, and when the group moves the secluding aura moves with it. The dance, which is also a ritual, resembles certain figures in the *Lancers*. They have a decided sense of rhythm, for although their movements are spontaneous and free they are to some extent " keeping time."

As I watch them, in the centre of the circle there has developed slowly a rose-coloured globular or heart-shaped form, whose pulsation discharges a force that flows out in fine lines or striations. The auric encasement has now increased considerably in size, and is not unlike a large inverted glass bowl. They seem to have the idea that they are creating a building, for now radial divisions appear, extremely thin and glittering, which divide the erection into compartments. Gradually the group drifts away out of the range of my vision.

Lancashire. 1921.

We are surrounded by a dancing group of lovely female fairies. They are laughing and full of joy. The leader in this case is a female figure, probably two feet high, surrounded by transparent flowing drapery. There is a star on her forehead, and she has large wings which glisten with pale, delicate shades from pink to lavender; in rapid movement, however, the effect of them is white. Her hair is light golden brown and, unlike that of the lesser fairies, streams behind her and merges with the flowing forces of her aura. The form is perfectly modelled and rounded, like that of a young girl, the right hand holds a wand. Although her expression is one of purity and ingenuousness, her face is at the same time stamped with a decided impression of power. This is especially noticeable in the clear blue eyes, which glow like flame and have all the appearance of a living fire. Her brow is broad and noble, her features small and rounded, the tiny ears are a poem of physical perfection. There are no angles in this transcendently beautiful form. The bearing of head, neck and shoulders is queenly, and the whole pose is a model of grace and beauty. A pale blue radiance surrounds this glorious creature, adding to her beauty, while golden flashes of light shoot and play round her head. The lower portion of the aura is shell pink, irradiated with white light.

She is aware of our presence and has graciously remained more or less motionless for the purpose of this description. She holds up her wand, which is about the length of her fore-arm and is white and shining and glows at the end with a yellow light. She bows low and gracefully, much as a great *prima donna* might bow on taking leave of a highly appreciative audience. I hear a very faint, far-away music, too fine-drawn to translate, such music as might be given forth by diminutive needles, delicately tuned, hung and struck with tiny hammers. It is more a series of tinkles than a consecutive air, probably because I am unable to contact it fully. Now the whole group has risen into the air and vanished.

CHAPTER VI

SYLPHS

THE term "sylph" is used in two ways: either to describe those nature-spirits which use the element of air more than of earth, fire, or water, or as denoting a particular stage in the deva evolution. By this I mean that, just as on the human line of evolution the life works up through the mineral, vegetable, and animal stages, and then moves on into the human kingdom and becomes an *individual human being,* so the stream of nature-spirit life evolves likewise through the mineral and vegetable and on to the animal world, where it is associated with the smaller birds, fishes and insects. The lesser fairies, etc., that we have described are about at the level of our domestic animals; and the life finally passes through these forms to that of the sylph, after which stage it is able to act as an individualised "angel." In this book, however, I have given the name of sylph only to those nature-spirits which appear to be connected with wind, cloud, and storm.

Bowland. July, 1921.

Revelling in the force of the wind, high up in the air, sylphs are to be seen. They are rather below human height, but quite human in form, though a-sexual. They are disporting themselves wildly in groups of two and three, travelling at great speed across the sky. There is a certain fierceness in their joy as they shriek to each other, their cries sounding like the wild whistling of the wind; they recall in this aspect the Valkyries of the Wagnerian " Ring."

At first sight they appear to be winged, with a pair of magnificent white pinions attached to their body from the top of the shoulders and reaching down to the feet; and one even seems to detect a regular formation within these wings, which is, however, an illusion, produced by the forces flowing through their auras. Pale rose and pale azure blue predominate, while the radiance of many hues plays continually about their heads. A group of three, which I am watching, presents a most spectacular appearance. As they wheel and fly across the wide arch of the heavens, the bright colourings flash forth with extreme rapidity, between them and about them in all directions, but more especially up into the air. Occasionally, what appears like a variegated sheet of colour, arranged in shining bands, streams from one to the other, and shades off into the palest tints imaginable, which, as far as I can see them, are chiefly pale blue, rose, green, and lavender, while through them scintillates a brilliance like yellow tongues of flame. There is a definite order in this colour communication, though the meaning of it is completely hidden from me; the chief notes seem to be fierce exultation and joy.

The faces of these creatures of the air are like strangely beautiful but fierce human females, strong, vital, and controlled in spite of their apparent reckless *abandon*. They appear to travel, with the speed of light, great distances, of ten to fifteen miles, in a moment of time. They are entirely astral in substance.

On the slopes of Helvellyn. April, 1922.
Watching the approach across the valley of some

dense storm-clouds, the presence was observed of a
number of bird-like air-spirits travelling swiftly in
front of the approaching clouds. Many of them are
dark and unpleasant to look upon—slightly reminiscent
of bats. They are darting backwards and forwards
across the valley, sometimes following the conformation
of the hills quite closely. They bring a condition of
high excitement with them, and give the impression that
they are working up the electric and magnetic conditions
which characterise a storm. Their faces are human and
well formed, their expression is unpleasant; the rest of
the body is not fully formed, and they rather resemble
birds with human faces. They travel with far greater
speed than would be possible for any bird, crossing the
valley in a second of time.

The direction of the clouds has now changed, and
they have swung over southwards on to a new front.
There are large numbers of them, probably a hundred,
and among them are some whiter varieties. They utter
a weird shrieking noise, and occasionally shoot almost
vertically upwards into and beyond the clouds. These
are not the powerful elementals that are generally seen
in the midst of a thunderstorm, which are much larger
and usually attract attention by brilliant points of yellow
light among the thunder clouds.

It is evident that there are many different species of
storm-sylphs, varying in size, power, and evolutionary
position.

STORM SPIRITS

During the Great Storm in London, 3 a.m.,
July 10th, 1923.

Demoniacal and terrific beyond description are the
beings who are to be seen exulting in the aerial regions

while the jagged flashes of the lightning and the deafening roar of the thunder continue hour after hour through the night.

Their appearance faintly suggests gigantic bats. Their bodies are human in shape, yet it is no human spirit which, brilliant as the lightning itself, shines through those large upward-slanting eyes. Black as the night is their colour, red and flame-like the aura which surrounds them, dividing into two huge pinions behind their bodies; hair, that is like a fire, streams back from the head as though in tongues of flame.

Thousands of beings, of whom this is but a halting description, revel in the midst of the storm. The clash of the mighty forces gives them an exaltation of consciousness (a word expressing the opposite extreme from " exaltation " would be more accurate, for the effect is to furnish those dark legions of the storm with conditions in which they can come forth into outward manifestation, by providing them with vehicles). They wheel, swoop, dart, soar and hover, apparently intensifying the forces of the storm, which in them seems to find embodiment.

Behind these and above them in the very heart of the storm is one beside whom the elementals of storm and disintegration are but flickering bats. There, in the heart of it all, is to be seen one of the great devas of the elements—human in form, yet utterly superhuman in beauty, majesty and power. It was the knowledge of this " Presence " in the midst which inspired courage and calmness when, just before a flash of lightning cleaved the heavens with a ribbon of fire, one of the dark beings seemed to swoop down, and for a moment hover close above us. The baleful eyes, gleaming with frenzy, were fixed upon the earth below.

For a fraction of a second the consciousness behind those eyes was contacted, producing a feeling of vertigo and terror such as had not been experienced since the dark days of the war and the awful nights passed under bomb and shell fire. Under this present test the value of those days was realised, for automatically the consciousness overcame the fear, and stilled the trembling of the body caused by the vision and the deafening crack of thunder by which it was accompanied. Instantly the dark storm-fiend sped away, uttering the weird, exulting, unearthly cry which was continually audible, as if from a thousand throats, throughout the storm.

In the midst of all this uproar there was calm, poise unshakable, a power which even these unruly legions acknowledged. Beyond a certain limit they could not go, for they were ever held in check by a Will which reigned supreme over the elemental forces as, like Hell let loose, they fought out the battle of the storm, hour after hour, through the night.

Geneva. 1924.

As I was watching the swift travelling of the sylphs high in the upper air, one of their number, pausing for a moment, approached us. He descended slowly, until he came to a condition of comparative rest at a height of about four feet from the ground, where he remained, a being of transcendent beauty, poised in the air, just above the tops of the waving grasses.

The form was nude, a-sexual but masculine in type, in stature about eight feet, perfectly modelled, beautifully proportioned. Surrounding it was an aura, about three times the size of the form, with radiations which extended much further beyond the periphery. The centre

of life appeared to be a *chakram* in the region of the
solar plexus, which was extremely active and marvellously
radiant. The colours of the aura appeared to emerge
from this centre and to flow in continuous waves outwards
to the edge. Highly complex forms were produced by
its rotatory motion and the emerging lines of force and
colour. All these lines were curved, and continually
recrossed each other like basket-work, and the whole
centre was spinning with great rapidity and shining
intensely.

The main colouring of the aura was gold and rose;
with this was mixed an unusual shade of blue, which,
combined with the other two colours, caused a purple
hue, like that of heather in sunlight, to flow continually
through the aura. In addition to this, lines of force
streamed away from the body, dividing at the shoulders
in a wing-like formation which extended above the head.

Contact with the consciousness of this glorious being
gave a sense of exaltation, radiance, and intense activity.

The play of its consciousness affected the aura over its
head, causing sets of colours, differing from those
described, to appear and disappear, keeping pace with the
activities of the mind.

It stretched its hands towards us, sending a stream of
energy into us, causing our auras to vibrate with a little
of its own force. Raising its hands and arms vertically
upwards, it seemed to appeal to us to leave the limitations
of the flesh and rise with it to higher levels of space and
consciousness. (As an attempt to surrender to the sum-
mons produced an intense pain in the head, we were
forced regretfully to decline the dangerous invitation.)

I realised that, even in those moments when we
experience joy and exaltation in the fullest measure
possible to us, we are still very far below the intense

and dazzling vividness of existence which is the normal condition of such an one as I have attempted to describe.

CLOUD FAIRIES

Grand Saleve. 1924.

Cloud fairies seem to combine the qualities of the undine and the sylph. They dwell in and around the cloud, the shape of which they seem to mould and to hold when moulded, modifying, by their form-building power, the shapes caused by the action of the wind. In the sunlit heart of the big clouds a wonderful atmosphere is produced, the fairies building for themselves palaces, castles, and all kinds of fairy dwelling-places. Occasionally, under the control of a high deva, a whole cloud will be moulded by their united co-operation. It is interesting to watch a small wisp of cloud detach itself and assume peculiar forms as of some weird animal, insect, bird or fish. One might almost regard the clouds as schools, as places of instruction in the handling of elemental essence and in the building of forms in preparation for the more difficult work in dense matter.

CHAPTER VII

DEVAS

To the Eastern mind the word "deva" refers to a host of "shining ones" of almost infinite variety of form and function. In this book I have confined myself to those particular classes which are especially associated with Nature and which I have had the opportunity of studying.

This chapter deals chiefly with the nature-devas concerned with the vegetable kingdom who, in most cases, are seen in the open country, away from human habitations.

To them physical bodily life has not the importance which we attach to it. They are accustomed to the destruction of form and would not discriminate between a wrecked human body and a lightning-riven tree.

They represent what might be termed *Nature's point of view*, and see in the destruction of form nothing more than a change—a natural process. It is impossible for this particular type of nature spirit to understand our human sentiments and valuations of form, while to human beings their utterly logical attitude appears as implacable ruthlessness. Another marked difference is shown by their disregard of detail, while human life is practically made up of details. The nature-deva deals in broad outlines, vast landscapes, and huge elemental forces, and never appears to consider a part as separate from the whole. They are the life side of Nature, an expression

of the Divine energy, and might almost be regarded as
Will-forms. The will of the Creator finds its expression
in them, and they are its agents and channels in manifested
Nature.

NATURE-DEVAS
Lake District. November, 1921.

I am impressed by the fact that the whole of this
district is densely populated with deva life at all levels
from that of the tiny nature-spirit, brownie, mannikin,
gnome, and fairy, up to the individualised orders of
nature-devas. Broadly speaking, the lower types remain
near the surface of the earth; there is a clan of fairies
apparently approaching individualisation and possessing
both intelligence and will-power, which rises to considerable heights; the upper air and mountain summits
are occupied by the various nature-devas; it would appear
that these last rarely descend to the bottom of the valley,
and much more frequently rise to great heights in the
air.

The first glimpse I get is that of swiftly moving forms
on the surface of the mountain and in the air. Sometimes it is possible to follow a single form for long distances; at other times the attention is attracted by a
vivid flash with a sense of movement in a definite direction only. It is something like the traffic of a populous
city, with the buildings and noise eliminated. No matter
where I look, or to what distance, I am aware of this
phenomenon.

A WHITE NATURE-DEVA
Lake District. June, 1922.

High up on the fell behind us I see several nature-
devas, whose chief colouring is white, their auras

resembling beautiful cirrus clouds. At first glance they appear to be clothed in flowing white robes, almost Grecian in style, which are in constant movement, as if blown by a high wind. The actual form is distinctly human, and in its appearance the female predominates. The features are rounded and soft, and the eyes are more kindly and less piercing in this particular type than is usual. The aura is of subtler matter than the robes, and is marvellously beautiful. The colours, which are extremely delicate, are apparently arranged concentrically; beginning from the outer edge the colours, so far as I can see them, are white, lavender, yellow, pink, and pale pink, with a slightly denser white aureole surrounding the actual form. All the colours are in most ethereal shades of delicate loveliness. The concentric arrangement is frequently changed, or covered by other colours which flash forth with the changes in consciousness.

From the top of the shoulders and head, starting from the periphery of the body, the aura streams upwards to a distance of three of four feet in fine radiating lines of force; this gives an extraordinarily vital and definitely non-human appearance; sparks and flashes of golden fire play around the head. When the attention of this being is definitely attracted, the eyes light up with extraordinary brilliance and concentrated intelligence. In other portions of the aura there are similar, but smaller, radiations of force, and in the case observed these are very noticeable round the feet, which are perfectly formed, uncovered and human in aspect; the total height of the body is from five to six feet, and the aura extends to about double the height and width of the central figure.

It is curious to note the sense of instability of form

which is conveyed, as if the whole were so delicate and subtle that it would melt away. There is a radiant centre in the forehead which shines out brilliantly white, also one at each side of the head, and one at the top; this last is golden yellow in colour, and from it vivid forces are flowing upwards. There is a centre at the throat, which is not so active. These, together with a very large *chakram* at the solar plexus, appear to be all the centres of vitality in this being. A circular motion is apparent at this distance (300 to 400 feet) at the solar plexus, and the movement can be seen to be clockwise; it is an extremely active vortex, whose purpose seems to be entirely that of absorption, and, *as I concentrate upon it, I am able to see right inside* it and even to feel the condition at this vital centre; it reminds me at once of an electric power house. At first it appeared to me as a cup-like depression with the entrance in front; a momentary contact with it must have raised my consciousness to a higher dimension, for, although still retaining its cup-like shape, it was open in all directions. This centre appears to absorb vitality, while the others appear to discharge it and to afford the means of self-expression.

Lake Deva

On the western shores of Thirlmere. June, 1922.

During an evening stroll I was attracted by a nature-deva which appeared poised over the lake with its gaze and attention focussed upon it as if to pierce to its very depths.

Though a-sexual, male characteristics predominated in its appearance. The general colouring was that of heather glowing in the sunset and deepening in places to dark crimson. The face was that of a beautiful youth, and although the features were strongly marked the effect was rounded and smooth, the cheek-bones were high, and the eyes very wide apart and slightly drawn upwards at the outer edge.

The whole aura streamed upwards from behind the body, which was poised in a semi-horizontal position as if upborne on a powerful wind from below.

He made sudden movements, darting off to some 200 or 300 yards away, and then remaining poised as before, still gazing intently into the lake upon which his whole consciousness seemed to be centred. He appeared to be connected with the evolution taking place beneath the surface, and there were lines of force flowing from his eyes and hands down into the waters of the lake. His attention was that of one who scans some minute detail with great concentration, so that nothing escapes his gaze, and for the last half-hour, since he was first observed, his concentration does not seem to have wavered for the fraction of a second. I get the impression that he serves a superior who is always present to his consciousness.

NATURE-DEVAS

In the Lake District. Mythburn, November 26th, 1921. Facing Helvellyn. Up the hillside—glorious sunshine—frosty.

On or near the summit of the hills on our right are to be seen a number of devas. They have the same joy in the processes of Nature which animates the nature-spirits; in them also it inspires a certain gaiety of demeanour, but not the frolicsomeness of the little folk: a deep-seated joyousness, amounting at times to ecstasy, is shown in their expression and in their atmosphere.

Their height varies from that of a man to apparently eight or ten feet, and their slim graceful figures are robed in the rich colours of the scenery amidst which they live. Brown, soft, deep green as of fir trees, golden yellows, and the lighter greens of the grass— all sublimated to their highest octaves—shine forth resplendent in the bodies of light in which they are visible. Other colours are constantly flashing between them as they converse.

The colony consists of probably a hundred devas. They all appear to vary slightly in colour. In some the rich browns predominate, in others the green, in some the golden yellow, with the other shades showing as subordinate hues.

Some of the smaller ones appear to have wings, or a semblance of them, but not the larger ones who live near the summit.

They move across the valley frequently in pairs, sometimes travelling with incredible rapidity, sometimes floating gracefully—even disporting themselves in the air.

Just now others arrived through the air, and while I was watching them, a much larger nature-spirit arose from a point several hundred feet up the hillside and flashed across the valley, an object of great beauty— though its movements were too swift for detailed description. It had a human female figure, very large wings, and must have been six or eight feet in height; its main colourings were bright red and gold. It travelled far more swiftly than any bird, while the lesser fairies appear to move at about a swift bird's pace.

These fells are the home of a large number of nature-devas. They first become visible to me as they leave the rocks, and I see them singly, or in pairs, or occasionally in larger groups, moving across the valley to the opposite hills. Sometimes they remain poised midway, at others they rise to great heights, and I have not seen any descend below 300 to 400 feet above the stream which flows murmuring at the foot of the hill. I also see these devas gliding about on the top of the crag, and now at last get a glimpse of one of which a more detailed description is possible.

It is a noble and beautiful female figure. As I first saw it, it remained poised for a moment facing in our direction, with feet together and arms outstretched, its auric robe appearing quite solid within the clearly defined inverted triangle formed by the fingertips and feet. Now it is forming itself into another symbol by raising its arms in graceful curves and joining the finger tips over the head; an inverted triangle with a circle resting on its upturned base is clearly seen, because the triangular auric condition is maintained by the will, although the position of the arms is changed. The face looking out through the circle adds to the force of this symbol. In the midst of the aura the denser lines of the body give a clear representation of the Egyptian Tau. The arms are now drawn together and extended horizontally from the body, the head being bowed between the arms. There must be some auric extension of the arms because, viewed from the side, an equilateral triangle standing on its point is formed. This pose has had the effect of concentrating the aura, which now appears to be much more dense, and the red colouring now predominates. These movements are extremely graceful and seem intended to convey some meaning connected with the manifestation of the forces of Nature. Other symbols are following, but my vision has become less clear, probably owing to a breakdown in concentration. The figure now appears to be whirling rapidly in that manner known to boys as the cartwheel: it thus forms a perfect circle, and during the movement the limbs show constantly as fixed radii. *(At this point I was unable to maintain my observation any longer.)*

A Crimson Nature-Deva at Close Quarters

Lake District. June, 1922.

After a scramble of several hundred feet up a rocky glen we turned out to one side, on to the open fell where it faces a huge crag. Immediately on reaching the open we became aware, with startling suddenness, of the presence of a great nature-deva, who appeared to be partly within the hillside.

My first impression was of a huge, brilliant crimson, bat-like thing, which fixed a pair of burning eyes upon me. The form was not concentrated into the true human shape, but was somehow spread out like a bat with a human face and eyes, and with wings outstretched over the mountainside. As soon as it felt itself to be observed it flashed into its proper shape, as if to confront us, fixed its piercing eyes upon us, and then sank into the hillside and disappeared. When first seen its aura must have covered several hundred feet of space, but in a later appearance, in which it again showed itself, the actual form was probably ten to twelve feet high. The auric flow was exceedingly beautiful and swept back behind the body in wing-like sheets, extending from the top of the head down to the

o

feet, and reaching backwards and outwards in graceful curves and flowing lines. The colours were darker than any of those I have yet seen in this type of being—a rich dark blue was the background of the auric colourings— with lighter blue, gold, pink, and leaf green also showing. In some parts the colours appeared almost like a peacock's feathers, in fact the aura was not unlike a glorified peacock's tail in effect.

There was a virility and force and an air of definite masculinity about this being. A continuous flow of the auric emanations caused ripples and waves to chase one another through the aura, suggesting coloured draperies in a very high wind. The central form and the central portion of the aura were of a rich crimson, the body actually glowing with this colour. He appeared to be "in charge" of that part of the landscape—to have undertaken its evolution, as it were—and his powerful vibrations were distinctly to be felt and must have a quickening effect upon the animal, vegetable, mineral and fairy life within his sphere of influence. This is the clearest vision I have ever had, and coming, as it did, quite unexpectedly, it carried with it powerful conviction to me. My physical body thrilled for hours afterwards with the force of the contact and the *rapport* established between us.

TREE-DEVAS

Thirlmere. February, 1922.

A group of very old firs growing on the site of the old Roman colony called "The City," on the western shores of Thirlmere, is seen to possess a very marked personality, and the same is true of several individual trees which give the impression of exceptional vigour and advancement, considerably beyond the normal for tree consciousness. There is nothing of the placidity of the oak, or of the slight restless awareness of the beech, but there is here an intensity of life, as though the ensouling consciousness had absorbed something of the fierceness of the elements, which this noble and ancient group has so long withstood.

This intensity of consciousness is considerably increased by the presence of a number of very active nature-spirits who appear to find in "The City" a responsive field for their labours; they are moving swiftly in and out among the trees, continuously impressing their vibrations upon them. So great is the power with which they express this vibration that it produces the psychic effect of a sound like the running of a well-tuned motor engine. Some of these nature-spirits appear to have associated themselves closely with an individual tree or a lesser group of trees, and to remain stationary with their charge or charges included within their auras. Others move about, at the height of the topmost branches of the trees, and though they occasionally rise further into the air they do not appear to descend to the ground.

I am again impressed with the virile intensity and ceaseless activity which characterise their work. They have succeeded in establishing a powerful keynote for the auric vibration of the whole group of trees, and it would seem that their continued presence is necessary if the quickening energising force thus induced is to be maintained. On the physical plane it manifests itself as a powerful magnetic influence, so marked as to be noticeable without the aid of clairvoyance.

The nature-spirits do not appear to be individualised as yet; they are manifestly working under a group consciousness. I am not able to see the forms below the level of the waist. In each the head and shoulders are distinctly human in appearance, but below that the form becomes indefinite, and so many streams of force play through it in different directions that it appears to shade off into auric activity; their auras contain numerous eddies and vortices, but the main streams of force suggest wing-like formations. The centre of life appears to be in the middle of the head, where there is a clearly defined *chakram*. The eyes are preternaturally bright, looking more like centres of force than organs of vision; they do not appear to be capable of seeing to any distance, and I question whether they are used for the recognition of any objects other than those with which they are immediately concerned. (The consciousness is seated at a higher level, and awareness is obtained by an inner sense rather than by " sight.") These particular nature-spirits do not seem to possess a high order of intelligence; although animated by a single purpose and having powers of concentration beyond those of the average human being, they are childlike and simple, possessing little or no mentality.

Preston. 1921.

As we walk along a field path a tall tree-deva has flashed into view some fifty yards ahead of us at a place opposite an old willow tree to which it appears to belong; the deva is silver in colour, and as tall as a human being. Having shown herself etherically by the flash which first attracted our attention, she now remains watching us from within the aura of the tree. (It is the aura which is silver, the body being flesh-coloured.) She has a protective, almost maternal, attitude towards the tree, and is not unfriendly to us. Her form is very beautiful, the arms particularly so, being long and very graceful, and her auric draperies remind one of falling water; she does not appear to be winged, though the waving streams of force suggest the contrary. With her rose-coloured lips and cheeks, and her very human smile, she has the ability to make herself appear like a flesh-clothed human woman.

The effort to contact her consciousness more closely threatens to bring me under that glamour which observers of Fairyland have so often recorded.

She seems to be conscious in all that portion of the tree which is above ground, her aura being larger than and including that of the tree, which she does not appear to have the desire to leave although she may have the ability to do so. I think she knows of the existence of the human family as neighbours, and regards the average passer-by with a certain good-natured indifference. There are many lower orders of nature-spirits connected with the tree, busily carrying out their various functions. While she is not the director of their efforts she is aware of them, and may occasionally control their activities.

Epping Forest. July, 1923.

This part of the forest is thickly populated with an exceptionally beautiful order of tree-spirits, differing in many respects from those we have met hitherto. One striking difference is that there appears to exist between them something like a communal feeling, in contrast to the aloofness and reserve of many other tree-devas. They are non-individualised, female in form; their main colouring is a shade of green, rather more emerald than that of the leaves, but without the vividness associated with emerald green; it is a soft green and does not glisten or shine, it is almost as though the surface was slightly rough; a golden brown, not dissimilar from the colouring of autumn leaves in sunshine, is mingled with this green.

Most of these tree-spirits wear the appearance of young girls, and are of human height. They have long dark hair, which hangs loose and gives them a rather wild look. Some are wearing garlands and loosely-hanging necklaces of leaves. The arms are bare and the shape from the waist downwards is not always clearly defined; one sees a downward flow of auric force, ethereal yet fairly stable, its colour like that of the tree trunks. I notice that when they move about among the trees, the lower limbs are clearly formed and gleam flesh-coloured through the auric garment; when floating they are folded together, and when on the ground are used normally, for walking, dancing, or posing. Their movements are most graceful as they glide and float among the trees. They are joyous, care-free, and communicative embodiments of the spirit of the forest.

A similar species remains in the higher branches, and of these only the head and shoulders are clearly formed; the rest of the body is continued in a sweeping auric robe, which gradually becomes so ethereal as to be merged in the surrounding atmosphere. Their heads are on a level with the tree-tops and their auras envelop the whole tree. The larger trees seem to have one each. In some cases their auras are extended to include the smaller trees, and where there is a closely grouped ring, two nature-spirits appear to have charge of the whole of it.

Closer scrutiny shows me that there are two different orders of tree-spirit, those described last being of a higher order, and possessing a much greater degree of consciousness. Their eyes are particularly brilliant and are set at an angle in the face. They are impassive, and possess a degree of poise to which their younger brethren have not yet attained. About the head their auric display is very radiant and contrasts with their rather sombre forest robes. Yellow, crimson and violet surround their heads in semi-circular concentric bands, which scintillate and flash into the upper air—again showing in marked contrast to the immobility of the denser form. On contacting one of them more closely I have become conscious of extreme age and unwearying patience. In their eyes is an inscrutable knowledge, a calm certainty, the reflection of a consciousness which, having seen the passage of earthly seasons without number, is content to remain, in order that the purposes of Nature may be fulfilled. Passing beyond the eyes into their consciousness one touches a vivid intensity which I can find no words to describe. To pass into theirs from our human brain consciousness might be compared to stepping out of water into fire. They seem utterly untouched and unaffected by the passage of time, as if our seasons were but days to them. Their consciousness is not focussed upon the physical plane, of which they seem little aware. They certainly pay no attention whatever to the human folk who pass beneath the leafy branches of the forest.

The dancing spirits first described are well aware of our presence and are by no means unfriendly. Occasionally they group themselves in a wonderful pose, remain motionless for a moment or two, and then resume their graceful movement. Some of their poses are fantastic and exaggerated in the extreme, others are purely Grecian; some are all graceful curves and flowing lines, others are angular and stiff. Their movements have none of the swift darting motion which one notices in so many nature-spirits. They move slowly, sinuously and gracefully, whether they are walking or floating.

There is here also a kind of faun, in height about two feet, somewhat like the traditional satyr, but without its ugliness. The upper part of the body is that of a young boy of about twelve or fourteen, while the lower resembles that of a deer. They have very prominent strongly marked features and a mischievous expression. The hair is curly. They prance around the tree-spirits, mimicking them, sometimes joining the group, but more usually merely playing about in a rather irresponsible way among the trees.

These phenomena appear to be bathed in a violet-grey light, an atmosphere which emanates from the earth and extends to a height of about eight or ten feet.

Lancashire. February, 1922.

The wood is composed of Scotch firs, birch, beech and ash, and is partially surrounded by a straggling and somewhat unkempt hawthorn hedge. It is the home of a small colony of very beautiful nature-spirits, apparently about twelve in number. They are of human height and form, but of no sex differentiation. Their main colouring is a bright apple-green, beginning at the shoulders with a very pale shade and deepening into a garment of dazzling beauty which streams far below their feet, like a long, diaphanous and iridescent train. The whole form shines with a similar brilliance of surface to that of a new green leaf. The upper part of the body is pale flesh colour, the face being of unusual beauty, and wearing an expression of great joy. This colony is at present extremely active, gliding and flashing up and down the wood, reminding one slightly of the appearance of bright fishes in a very clear stream, which occasionally turn on their sides and reflect gleams of light. The whole glade thrills with the presence of these beautiful beings: they remain about forty feet from the ground, and fly, with swift undulations, from end to end of the wood, and are impressing it with a definite rate of vibration, a strong magnetic impulse, by their long-continued and repeated activity. They are working to establish these vibrations permanently, and their efforts cause constant ripples and waves of brilliant rose, yellow, silver, and pale grass-green within the aura of the wood. They appear to have insulated the grove, placing it in a magnetic seclusion maintained by an etheric wall which they have built round it.

Two of them have observed us and paused in their rapid flight: they have focused their attention upon us and I feel the magnetic thrill which results from the impact of their consciousness. They are communicating with a helper who stands behind us, and who first directed our attention to the work; his poise and general air of quietness and stability is in strong contrast to the activity of these highly electric creatures.

At this moment a third nature-spirit has paused on the edge of the wood, about thirty yards away, and is regarding us with a radiant, dazzling smile. The auric flow in all these creatures is downwards and outwards from the shoulders: this is what gives the appearance of streaming train-like garments of glistening green. The flow of forces is clearly visible, showing as a golden iridescence within the green which follows and indicates the line of flow. The arms appear unusually long and of exceptional beauty, and are given a graceful waving motion during flight.

High up in the air above (perhaps 1,000 yards) is another group with whom these are connected, but beyond getting a sense of moving figures, bathed in colours faintly resembling the colours of a golden sunset, I am unable to contact them. Evidently this spot is an important centre of nature-spirit and deva life, and is being magnetised by them for some special purpose.

DEVA OF PINE FOREST

In a wood near Celigny, Geneva.
Friday, June 13th, 1924.

Whilst I have been watching the fairies and gnomes, with which this place abounds, a deva connected with the forest has appeared on the opposite edge of the clearing. He is specially connected with the fir trees, amid which he stands. It is interesting to note that while I am studying him a group of sylphs have passed over the top of the trees. He looked up at them and across at us as if to ask whether we saw them. He is very much at home among the trees and has a proprietary air with regard to them, and in his clothing—or rather in that part of his aura which resembles clothing —there are fringes and formations like the hanging needles of the fir trees. Over his head is a very bright band of brilliant colours, and these, combined with the fringes, produce the appearance of an American Indian, with head-feathers and fringed clothing.* I feel

---

* It seems reasonable to assume that the dyed head-feathers of the Indians are copied from these auras of nature-spirits which they resemble.

assured that he has been here since remote times, when the place was wild and uninhabited; also that he has seen the passing of many races of men. He seems much more familiar with mankind than most devas and communicates quite easily. It seems to be specially characteristic of this country that the human and deva kingdoms are exceedingly close together: I feel that the devas are less remote and that communication is easier.

He is showing me a little of his method of work. He has the faculty of expanding his aura to a very great extent, so that he can include within it numbers of the trees. He places himself near them, draws into himself, by a process rather like deep breathing, a special quantity of natural energy, concentrating his aura round the group of trees upon which he wishes to work, and then releases his force with a highly stimulating effect: this quickens the activity of the nature-spirits, and stimulates and arouses the developing consciousness evolving through the trees.*

When he is moving through space he arranges his auric forces so that they stream behind him, presumably in order that they should offer a minimum of resistance to his movement. As he comes to rest, his aura gradually adjusts itself to the normal, and one receives distinctly the impression of large wings. He does not use these auric wings for flight, their appearance being produced by the way in which he arranges the currents of force which play through his aura.

He now brings forward from the wood a beautiful nature-spirit, like a lovely young girl, in thin white

---

* This stimulation appears to draw down a response from the monadic triads into the group soul through the permanent atoms. See *A Study in Consciousness*, by Annie Besant.

drapery through which the form can be seen. He called her from the wood, holding out his left hand, and she floated gracefully towards him and grasped the outstretched hand with evident joy, but also with a kind of submission. Undoubtedly there is a measure of affection between them, suggesting the human relationship of parent and child, but containing also something of comradeship. She is connected with one of the trees, some part of its psychic constitution entering into her, and the connection between it and her is maintained during the time of separation; on being released by the deva she at once slipped back into the aura of magnetic seclusion which the tree provides. I gather that she is a tree-spirit.

There is some peculiar kind of gnome here, which floats about with its long shapeless legs trailing in the grasses; it is of a dark brown colour with a homogeneous body of spongy texture. Its arms end in a kind of clenched fist and its feet in points. The face is dark and swarthy, and its whole vibration rather weird and unearthly. A sensitive person approaching this place at night would feel this vibration.

There is also, at the root of the trees, an interesting variety of wood-elves, a group of which are regarding us with frank curiosity about twenty yards on our left. They have large heads and large pointed ears which stick out at the sides of the head. Their bodies are too small for the size of their heads, and their expression displays a mentality very low down in the scale. They scamper and play about amongst the dead leaves, occasionally joining in a curious dance-like movement, in which they will form a ring and, with joined hands, encircle a tree or a group of trees. They seem to inhabit the roots of the trees for I see them emerge from the roots at the level of the ground as one would step out of the door of a house.

At Nateby, Lancashire. September 1st, 1922.

This is a small oblong wood of well-grown ash and elm, about half an acre in extent. It differs from those hitherto studied by reason of the fact that it is inhabited by only one nature-spirit, whose working methods are also unusual. This is a deva of considerable development which performs its function upon the wood from a position in space some fifty to 100 yards above the tree tops.

Though asexual, the form is predominatingly masculine. The chief colourings are bright carmine and gold; the face is singularly beautiful, the eyes brilliant and dark; the shape of the body below the shoulders is lost in the strong downward flow of the aura, which envelops the whole wood, enclosing it in an auric insulation. Within this there appears to be an upward flow into the centre of the deva's aura; psychically the whole looks solid, the space within the auric envelope being completely filled with fine flowing forces.

The deva remains relatively motionless and, judging by the expression of its eyes, is extremely alert and observant. Occasionally it directs the flowing forces by movements of its arms, the whole presenting one of the most beautiful and extraordinary sights I have seen.

The aura proper of the deva spreads out in a wonderful ovoid of brilliant hues, those mentioned predominating, for some hundreds of feet above the ground: it radiates and scintillates like the *aurora borealis*, while the lower portion, which enfolds the wood, sweeps down in graceful curves and is coloured carmine, with fine sprays of golden sparks following the downward sweep.

The dimensions may be of interest: from the ground to the highest point of the aura is about 150 feet, and the envelope of the wood eighty yards by thirty yards, approximately.

NATIONAL DEVAS
A Manx National Deva

The Isle of Man. Lake District. August, 1922.

I became conscious of the presence, at no great distance, of a god of majestic appearance and mighty power. He stands somewhere on the hill-top, with head slightly bowed, looking down upon the island over which he presumably presides. On his kingly head rests a five-pointed crown, consisting of a thick band with five points arising from it at intervals round the head, one appearing over each temple. In his right hand he bears a staff or thyrsus; his figure is gigantic and herculean, suggesting tremendous, almost resistless, strength. The general appearance is dark to me, but this may be caused either by my inability to see him clearly, or by distance. He stands motionless, as if watching and waiting, in a state of mental alertness, and his consciousness is obviously concentrated at levels above and beyond that of the traditional form which I glimpse. Undoubtedly there is a magnetic, not to say spiritual, connection between this country and Ireland, and the figure described appears to represent the spiritual forces of that ancient land—to be an outpost of the spiritual consciousness of Ireland. He appears to be a high deva, with special powers over the elements (a sort of Manx *Jupiter Pluvius et Tonans*). I should place him as a presiding genius, a national deva, an ancient ruler of this land. Yet in some ways he seems to be connected more with the island itself, and all its varied natural conditions and non-human inhabitants, than with its people, though these also are within the grasp of his consciousness.

In some fashion, hard to express, I am conscious of the existence of a still more mighty being in Ireland, the head of a hierarchy of spiritual intelligences to which the being described belongs. That he has his agents among the lesser order of nature-spirits is apparent, and I should place the devas seen on the summit of Snaefell in that category. An attempt to contact his consciousness produces not, as I expected, a greater realisation of his nature, but visions of the past history of this island, which form part of his memory.

I see a tall, powerful, viking-like race of men on the hillsides, making their way from their ships which lie on the north-east shores, towards Snaefell, as if summoned to a gathering. They are fair and powerfully built. Their clothing is of skins, their hair is long and their speech guttural and harsh. Another group of dark swarthy men approach from the south-west and south of the island, and it is obvious from this plane of consciousness, that there has been much bloody warfare between them in the remote past. The island in those days was larger than it is now and was occupied by at least two different races or types, and its connection, both spiritual and material, with Ireland was much closer than with England.*

* Tradition tells of a reigning deity called Manaan, a divine king, under whom were non-human servants, known as " hosts," whose appearance corresponds in some particulars to that of the Deva described on the summit of Snaefell.

The God of Helvellyn

June, 1922.

There is a mighty Being whose abode is the mountain Helvellyn. He appears to me as a seated figure of human shape and enormous proportions. In endeavouring to study him, I find myself without any canons whereby his stature and his life may be apprehended. He appears motionless, and yet suggests great activity. He is quiescent, and yet obviously the unquestioned ruler of the life side of the mountain's existence. At the level of consciousness at which I am able to perceive him, the limitations of geographical space have no power, so that while from one point of view his form appears to be *within* the mountain's mighty mass, yet from another his head appears to reach up to the clouds.

His immediate auric emanations are like no others I have seen; they consist of a large number of pointed tongues of flame, which radiate from him in all directions, reaching to great distances. Though these distances are beyond my conception of actual measurement, I should guess that they reach to at least 400 or 500 yards in all directions from his form, which is situated somewhere near the centre and summit of the Helvellyn group; beyond these striations his aura extends practically over the whole mountain, whose girth is said to be forty miles. Such an extension can hardly be correctly described as an aura; it is rather the sphere of influence within which he can act instantly.

He appears as if seated in profound meditation, motionless and expressionless save that the eyes are ablaze with power—the power of a highly unfolded and awakened consciousness. Even at this distance (of three miles) they produce a decided effect upon my consciousness. They glow like twin lakes of fire. His consciousness is seated in the eternal, and appears as deep-rooted and unshakable as the very mass of the mountain on which he resides. He remains motionless, firm as the mountain itself. From him great spiritual forces are flowing, radiating through his aura and out into space. He is surrounded by lesser devas and nature-spirits, aerial beings, whose movements give one the impression that they are in some cases messengers and in others servants, though I see no sign either of the receipt or despatch of a message or an order from the motionless God round whom this wondrous play of devic life is centred.

The summit, Grand Saleve, Switzerland.
June 10th 1924.

Poised high in the heavens above the mighty peaks is to be seen the form of a great angel, who might well be taken for the national deva of Switzerland. From the thought-forms surrounding and moulding its appearance on the lower levels it appears to be a member of the deva hierarchy, which occupies the position of ruler and guide.

The Swiss national thought-form, of a great figure with a red shield upon which appears a white cross, is ensouled by this being, and it is in this guise that I see him now standing motionless in space, at a point which appears to be about three times the height of the Dent du Midi. He is a wonderful being of enormous stature and, though I have no means of comparison by which to estimate it with accuracy, he seems to be at least twenty feet high. His gaze is compassionate, calm, beneficent;

around his head numbers of lesser devas are to be seen in constant motion, arriving and departing continuously; probably they are messengers to and from the various cantons, cities and villages.

This deva differs from any I have hitherto seen in that his vibration is less remote from our own and his intellectual activities are distinctly akin to the human; in addition, there is a remarkable quality of compassion, and the most intimate understanding of humanity, which certainly has not been the case with those members of the deva kingdom contacted hitherto; further, there is not that sense of bodily and auric activity, of out-rushing force which characterises the nature-devas; on the contrary there is a wonderful calm, a stillness as of the mountains themselves, except in the eyes and around the head, where ceaselessly there plays a vibration like multi-coloured tongues of flame. From another point of view it might be said that the entire country is embraced in his aura, which sweeps downwards and, as it descends, expands to include the whole extent of his great charge.

CHAPTER VIII

THE descriptions which follow give some idea of the appearance and nature of artificial entities created by the practice of magic, as well as of those true nature-spirits who assist at and take part in ceremonial worship.

ELEMENTARY

Whitendale. April, 1922.

" Buried in the hillside up to its shoulders was seen an elementary of human shape. Entirely black in colour, with a satanic cast of feature, it more nearly resembled the orthodox devil than anything I have ever seen. It seemed to be a prisoner in the earth, above which its head, shoulders and arms were visible. Its face wore a fiendish, leering grin, and it was struggling to become free. It gave the impression of extreme age and diminished vitality. It was an elemental relic of ancient magic rites. In those distant days it was free, an evil demon, in the form of a gigantic vampire. It was created and employed by a company of priests, worshippers of the ' Lords of the dark face,' to perform their evil designs.

I glimpse, from the remote past, weird and unholy ceremonial practices, which were performed in this

* These have been described by the Rt. Rev. Bishop C. W. Leadbeater in his *Science of the Sacraments.*

neighbourhood. Surrounding a group of magicians are numbers of lesser elementaries, all quite black in colour, over whom the being above described appears to rule. These lesser demons are in constant motion, travelling from and returning to the circle. The conditions of this worship are too horrible to describe and, even at this remote distance in time, the awful influence and appalling stench of their ceremonial remains in the astral light. They literally wallowed in blood and horror.

The lower portion of the body, more particularly the feet, of the imprisoned elementary are even yet immersed in emanations and conditions produced by blood ceremonial. This creature is doomed to disintegration, against which he is fighting with all that remains of his fast fading energy. For thousands of years this process has been going on, the etheric double of the form slowly rotting from the feet upwards. Unless the disintegration is artificially hastened it would appear that many hundreds of years must yet pass before the vile spirit imprisoned there is wholly released. The form, which resembles a huge pitch-black man, was artificially created by means of bloody rites and ceremonial magic. It is human in shape and yet inhuman; for it has a tail and the feet have but two huge toes. It is with great relief that I turn from this study to the charming and kindly little folk, romping, flying and running about the heather-clad hillside."

ELEMENTARY

In the fields near Preston. September, 1921.

" An unpleasant elementary has been watching us for some time from a distance of ten yards on our left.

I judge it to be an artificially-created entity which is probably a relic of the witchcraft which had such a hold on this country during the seventeenth and eighteenth centuries.

Its appearance and expression constantly vary in response to the activities of a sort of automatic mentality which was impressed upon it by its creator.

When first seen, it appeared with a very large head and face and a very small body and limbs; it wears a pointed cap and its face is intensely ugly and inhuman in expression. Closer inspection shows that it has a very red face, and a large mouth, in which there are a few decayed teeth, set permanently in an ugly and malicious grin. The form is bent and aged, and it appears to totter with weakness when manifesting in its present etheric form, in which it attains the extreme of density and outward manifestation possible for it. The decaying vegetation, garbage, and driftwood of the brook offer it conditions in which it is able to prolong its existence.

Before noticing it I had been watching the gambols of some little elves under a tree, and the contrast between their natural beauty and purity and the malicious ugliness of the elementary was very marked.

Leaning on its staff it staggers over the grass toward the elves, who stop their games and gather together in groups as it approaches. Its attitude towards them is obviously hostile. Happily it is quite powerless to hurt them. It might well strike horror into the heart of any human being who chanced to contact it and to realise its unpleasant nature.

As I watch it, its form becomes less dense and increases to normal human size and shape; it looks much like the traditional witch. Suddenly it mounts its stick, astride of which it rises into the air, and floats off, cackling as it passes out of my sight."

NATURE-SPIRITS SEEN AT A MASS CELEBRATED IN THE COUNTRY

Harpenden. 1924.

During the celebration of Mass I became aware that nature-spirits of many kinds approached and hovered in a great radiant cloud in the air immediately within reach of the vibrations of the ceremony. The smaller creatures—fairies, tree spirits and some manikins—bathed in the atmosphere of power with continuous and graceful motion. The higher and more evolved members of our hidden congregation remained relatively motionless, watching, and absorbing the force poured out, and adding enormously to the purity and beauty of the service. From the very beginning to the final blessing they shared the ceremony with us, and at its conclusion slowly melted away as they returned to their homes—in the trees, the cornfields, hedges and flowers,—taking with them, each according to his capacity, something of the blessing we had received.

In addition to these fairy people who came to church with us there were also present those orders of ceremonial angels who are definitely connected with the Mass.*

A DRUID CIRCLE

August, 1922.

(While attempting to study the fairy inhabitants of the English Lake district, a visit was paid to the Druid's

* See footnote, p. 115.

Circle, situated near Keswick. The incidents described
below appeared to be so vividly impressed upon the place
that I decided to try to describe those which seemed to be
within the reach of my vision, instead of studying the
normal fairy life of the district.)

" This is a complete Druid circle, consisting of single
stones, varying in height from one foot to six feet, and
surrounded on every side, except on the east, by
mountains.

Standing out vividly, against the background of many
strange scenes which pass before the inner eye, is the
impression made upon the place by the powerful personality of one man. A mighty figure, priest, teacher
and healer of his people, he stands out, like one of those
rugged heroes of antiquity one reads of in the stories of
ancient days.

He is above the average in stature, dignified and
impressive, with long dark hair and beard, which, later,
became pure white; he is robed in a single white garment, reaching to his feet, not unlike the surplice of
to-day. I see him standing here, where we are now
seated, within the inner circle of rocks; behind him is
a group of priests, robed as he is. Draped over tall
rocks, which have now disappeared, is a banner of pure
white, on which is worked a golden serpent. A large
concourse of people stands at some distance outside
the outer circle, as if waiting for a signal. The high
priest, who is evidently a master magician, raises both
hands to the heavens above him, lifts up his eyes and
utters a loud call. Hovering in the air are a number of
devas of various grades, and, at his call, six or seven of
the largest of them form a circle over his head some
80 or 100 feet in the air; their hands meet in the centre

bearing fire, which is materialised so as to be visible to physical sight.

A noticeable feature about these larger devas is that each one is wearing a crown, consisting of a narrow fillet of gold, encircling the head, in which are set dazzlingly bright jewels; at various positions round the head this fillet widens to upward points, a group of larger points resting over the forehead.

The fire descends upon the altar stone in front of the high priest, and burns brightly without visible sustenance. The other priests then form into two ranks and march forward to the altar stone, chanting a low and rather guttural hymn. On the descent of the fire the people form themselves into columns facing the three entrances at the north, south and west, and then march forward till they almost meet in the centre of the circle, leaving a fairly large square unoccupied. The people and the priests, with the exception of the high priest, then make obeisance to the fire; they stretch their arms forward and bow their heads, remaining in this position while the high priest utters a long prayer. A very powerful magnetic insulation existed, and still exists to some extent, round the circle, giving quite as much seclusion, from the occult point of view, as would a complete and solid temple. As the people stand with their heads bowed the devas descend quite close to them and a force, not unlike lightning in appearance, plays along their backs in the form of a huge cross. Lesser nature-spirits occupy the spaces in between the arms of this cross, some of them, as workers, holding the force along the lines of the cross, others apparently quite as much part of the congregation as the human beings. The priest evidently is conscious of the existence of some mighty spiritual entity, to whom he is praying and from whom the response apparently comes. This may be a *nirmanakaya** or a lofty deva, and the reservoir from which the power flows, and over which the being apparently has charge, appears to be situated high up in the heavens vertically over the temple.

The effect of the prayer is remarkable; the very heavens appear to open, and an enormous downrush of force pours into the central square formed by the people on three sides and the altar stones on the fourth. The people again stand erect, and the devas become intensely active, their chief concern being to see that the maximum of this force reaches the people, with a minimum of overflow and waste. The down-flow continues for some time, forming a veritable pillar of living power, whose appearance I am at a loss to describe, as any words of mine would inevitably fail. The nearest description I can give is to liken it to liquid, fiery mother-of-pearl, opalescent and tinged with an inner colouring of rose. It penetrates downwards far into the ground and reaches upwards out of sight into the heavens. The high priest plainly sees it, as do some of the priests; the people feel its presence, but few appear to see anything. All adopt a highly reverent attitude of mind and body, and realise the sacred nature of the occasion.

At a given signal from the high priest a number of sick and old people are carried into the spaces between the arms of the cross formed by the congregation; they are then led or carried into the square, where those who cannot stand are laid upon the grass, just outside the pillar of force. The weather is cold, and some of the

* Adepts, " Lords of Compassion," who sacrifice their beatitude (Nirvana) in order to help humanity. (Hoult's Glossary.)

sick and aged appear to have been suffering from this. The position they now occupy, however, greatly improves their condition. I see one man, of old and decrepit appearance, who was laid at the northern side of the square, raising himself on his right elbow, and extending his left hand towards the pillar, like one warming himself at a fire. A glow of heat and magnetic energy passes through his frame, his eyes light up, and after a few moments he rises to his knees, where he remains, still a tottering figure, but marvellously improved in both mind and body. He holds out the palms of his hands like a cup, into which one of the priests pours a little pale yellow liquid, which the old man drinks. Many others, men, women and children, receive such liquid. In cases of wounds the high priest heals them instantaneously by merely passing his hands over them. A tremendous power is flowing through him, his body appearing to be illuminated throughout with golden light; he evidently knows much of the inner powers of man, and his touch has a magical effect upon his patients. This portion of the ceremony lasts probably from twenty minutes to half an hour, after which the whole attention is focussed on the high priest, who, standing on a flat stone, delivers an exhortation. I cannot grasp a word of his utterance, but the main idea appears to be an appeal for the humanities and an endeavour to assist the people to realise their unity and interdependence. There are some rough, wild spirits amongst them who, although tamed for the time being by his power and that of the ceremony, are by no means so gentle and submissive in the fastnesses from which they have come.

Having concluded his discourse, he led the people in thanksgiving, all together making three obeisances like the one performed at the beginning. At the third, while the gathering remained with heads bowed, the high priest again looked up to Heaven and spoke; the downflow of power ceased quite suddenly, and the pillar disappeared. The people then turned about and, chanting with the priest, walked out of the circle by the entrances which had admitted them. They broke formation outside the circle and waited. The high priest then turned towards the serpent symbol and the priests who were facing him. He spoke to them and blessed them, swiftly making with his hand certain symbols in the air, which seemed to be of a circular or spiral nature, and which remained visible as they passed from his hand into the auras of the priests. He then extended his arms before him, partly open, as if to embrace the company of priests. They bowed their heads and a stream of power flowed from him to them and to the banner; this was maintained for an appreciable time, maybe ten seconds, during which the priests were lifted into a state of great exaltation; the banner was then rolled up, and the priests passed out of the inner circle, talking to those whom they knew, and, in some cases, moving off with them, as they gradually dispersed. The high priest, however, and some of the others, together with a few of the congregation who were apparently attached to his person, proceeded down the slope to the east, where there was a group of stone dwellings at the foot of the hill. Each person appeared to have a small cell of his own, in which was a rough bed of earth and peat. The windows were openings in the wall and the whole place decidedly primitive, though not uncomfortable. The high priest, immediately on entering his compartment, seated himself on a bench, and became entranced; he seemed to remain in this

state for a long time, doubtless his consciousness was freed
from the body.

The country all around was much wilder and bleaker
than it is at present, and there was a good deal of warfare
continually going on in different parts, as a result of
marauding excursions by surrounding tribes. It would
seem that some of the wounds healed during the ceremony
had been received in these encounters.

Evidently there were many ceremonies at which the
priests alone were present. I see them, standing in the
inner circle, saluting the rising sun. On another occasion
a ceremony is being performed at night, beneath the star-
lit sky, when the attention of the company is directed
to a brilliant star, low on the north-western horizon. I
notice, also, some system of signalling in operation, for
there are people on the summits of Skiddaw and Blen-
cathra and Helvellyn whose attention is directed to the
circle from which their signals are plainly visible.
Apparently beacon fires were used.

A system of contemplative discipline was evidently
employed by the priests, some of whom possessed the
power of self-entrancement. This temple appears to be
in magnetic contact with a centre of the same religion
lying to the south west, and a great way off.

At a later period, when only the memory of this priest
remained, he was worshipped almost as a deity by succeed-
ing generations, who regarded him as the master and
founder of their temple and its worship. A mighty white
magician apparently he was, as well as a teacher and lover
of his people. I see him, at a date much later than the
ceremony, a very old, but still perfectly upright, white-
headed figure, supported by two priests, making slow
progress from his dwelling up to the temple, where a
much bigger concourse of people is gathered together.

They greet him with a great shout, waving their arms with sticks and weapons in the air. Their shouting dies down to a murmur as he approaches the altar, and in a low voice he blesses them, stretching forth his right hand and waving it slowly over the crowd within the circle, beginning at the south and passing slowly round through the west to the north. All heads are bowed and the whole place becomes perfectly still, and when they look up again he has travelled some distance on his return to his dwelling-place; they watch him with hungry eyes, realising that they have seen him for the last time. Powerful emotion surges through them, many burst into tears and call after him.

Among his priests are some young men of exceptional character to whom he has imparted much of his mystic nature lore, and into whose hands is given the task of carrying on the temple worship and ministration after the master has left them.

How different is the scene before us now. The sun is setting in a golden glow, the quiet peace of a summer evening is broken only by the distant weird calling of the curlew and the cries of the numbers of young lambs who, with their mothers, are gazing in and about the ancient ring. Much of the old magnetic influence remains and can be felt; so strongly impressed on the place are the ancient ceremonies that they rise up continually before the inner eye.

Other scenes, far less holy and beautiful, have been enacted here, other priests of dark and fierce aspect have stood within the inner ring. One fierce viking-like figure, wearing a helmet with two horns upreared on each side of his brow, stands with bloody knife beside the altar stone. Dread now has taken the place of reverential awe in the hearts and minds of the congregation, and hatred has taken the place of love. No longer does blessing from on high pour down upon them. Now it is a power from below, which rises as if from the centre of the earth in answer to the invoking call; ugly as sin are the elemental shapes which hover round the ceremonial of blood. Women now live with men down at the ancient monastery, and the pure discipline and self-restraint of other days are gone.

In later times this ring, once the centre of such lofty ministrations, was foully desecrated by the followers of the 'Lords of the Dark Face,' and still clearly to be felt here is the scene of carnage which followed on the uprising of the surrounding tribes against the iniquities by which they had been overawed for many generations. The priests and priestesses were slain, victims were set free, and in their fury the mob demolished the dwellings at the foot of the hill and overthrew many of the temple stones.

Down through the thousands of years which follow, it is the first, the nobler, the uplifting influence which lasts and which is the most strongly impressed upon the place, showing something of the grandeur of the religion of ancient days."